Key Wo.
A Journal of Cultural Ma

8
(2010)

edited by
**Catherine Clay
Simon Dentith
Kristin Ewins
Ben Harker
Claire Jowitt
Angela Kershaw
Dave Laing
Stan Smith
Vicki Whittaker**

Key Words: A Journal of Cultural Materialism

Editors: Catherine Clay (Nottingham Trent University), Simon Dentith (University of Reading), Kristin Ewins (University of Salford), Ben Harker (University of Salford), Claire Jowitt (Nottingham Trent University), Angela Kershaw (University of Birmingham), Dave Laing (University of Liverpool), Stan Smith (Nottingham Trent University), Vicki Whittaker.

Guest editors for this issue: Tim Burke and John Goodridge (Nottingham Trent University).

Editorial Advisory Board: John Brannigan (University College Dublin), Peter Brooker (University of Sussex), Terry Eagleton (National University of Ireland Galway and Lancaster University), John Higgins (University of Cape Town), Andreas Huyssen (Columbia University, New York), John Lucas (Nottingham Trent University and Loughborough University), Peter Marks (University of Sydney), Sean Matthews (University of Nottingham), Jim McGuigan (Loughborough University), Andrew Milner (Monash University), Meaghan Morris (Lingnan University), Morag Shiach (Queen Mary, University of London), Dai Smith (Swansea University), Nick Stevenson (University of Nottingham), John Storey (University of Sunderland), Will Straw (McGill University), Jenny Bourne Taylor (University of Sussex), Jeff Wallace (University of Glamorgan), Imelda Whelehan (De Montfort University).

Contributions for prospective inclusion in *Key Words* should comply with the style notes printed on pp. 139–41 of this issue, and should be sent to Catherine Clay, School of Arts and Humanities, Nottingham Trent University, Clifton Campus, Nottingham NG11 8NS, United Kingdom (catherine.clay@ntu.ac.uk).
Books and other items for review should be sent to Professor J. Birkett, Treasurer, Raymond Williams Society, Department of French Studies, University of Birmingham, Birmingham, B15 2TT, UK.

Key Words is a publication of The Raymond Williams Society (website: **www.raymondwilliams.co.uk**).

Contributions copyright © The Raymond Williams Society 2010.

All rights reserved.

Cover design by Andrew Dawson.

Printed by Russell Press, Nottingham.
Distributed by Spokesman Books, Nottingham.

ISSN: 1369-9725
ISBN: 978-0-9531503-5-9

Contents

Editors' Preface	5
Guest Editors' Introduction **Retrieval and Beyond: Labouring-Class Writing** Tim Burke and John Goodridge	8
Brute Strength: Labouring-Class Studies and Animal Studies Donna Landry	15
Close Reading Yearsley David Fairer	18
Not So Lowly Bards: Working-Class Women Poets and Middle-Class Expectations Florence Boos	21
Genre Matters: Attending to Form and Convention in Eighteenth-Century Labouring-Class Poetry William J. Christmas	38
Ecocriticism Anne Milne	46
The Rise of Robert Bloomfield Scott McEathron	48
***The Foresters*: Alexander Wilson's Transatlantic Labouring-Class Nature Poetry** Bridget Keegan	51
'Tracing the Ramifications of the Democratic Principle': Literary Criticism and Theory in the *Chartist Circular* Mike Sanders	62
Labour History by Other Means Jonathan Rose	73

Contents

Graphic Bric-a-brac: Comic Visual Culture and the Study of Early Victorian Lower-Class Urban Culture 76
Brian Maidment

* * *

Language and Locale: John Locke, Somerset and Plain Style 94
Olivia Smith

Institutional Culture as Whiteness: 'a complex argument' 109
John Higgins

Reviews 127

Raymond Williams Foundation 138

Style Notes for Contributors 139

Editors' Preface

Throughout his long career as a critic and author Raymond Williams was interested in the complex ways economic reality shapes the imagination, and it is easy to see that *Key Words* 8, which is given over in part to a consideration of new directions in labouring-class studies, follows closely the cultural materialist critique he was so influential in developing. Williams consistently identified with the working classes, and was hostile to elitism in all its forms, evident in his account of his early days as an undergraduate in Cambridge – given much later in his 1958 essay 'Culture is Ordinary' – that he was 'in no mood, as I walked about Cambridge, to feel glad that I had been thought deserving; I was no better and no worse than the people I came from [...] because of this I got angry at my friends' talk about the ignorant masses'.[1] There is a persistent interest, discernible in all his writing from prentice work in the early 1950s until his death in 1988, in 'ordinary' people.

In broad terms *Key Words*' mission statement can perhaps be summed up as the development of Williams's formulation of a cultural materialist project 'always subject to redefinition': the essays, short pieces, and reviews published in this volume of the journal are united in recognising, as Williams did, that historical forces, cultural forms, and social, political and ideological themes and discourses all alter over time. But if Williams thought that the future would always be more complex than the present, the material guest-edited in this issue by Tim Burke and John Goodridge on eighteenth and nineteenth-century labouring-class writing reveals that the past was more intricate and nuanced than he sometimes allowed. For instance, Robert Bloomfield – celebrated here in Scott McEathron's short account of 'The Rise of Robert Bloomfield' – was not a poet Williams admired, preferring instead John Clare, whose work he championed in *The Country and the City* (1973). Yet Williams's influence and ideas are apparent everywhere in the essays Burke and Goodridge have edited. Recovery research is slowly filling in the gaps and fissures in our understanding of literary history, and questioning and opening out to scrutiny dominant assumptions about the past. The essays included here – on topics as various and stimulating as the ways 'land' was understood and represented by labouring-class writers in Britain and overseas, the relationship between genre and labouring-class writing, gender and genre in labouring women's writing, plebeian writing and visual culture, and working-class literary criticism – are by some of the most internationally significant scholars currently working in the field. In addition, five shorter pieces by leaders in their areas, which comment on particular individuals, or address key, emergent or urgent issues in this field, are interspersed amongst the longer essays. (See the separate introduction to this material by Burke and Goodridge.)

Two further essays included in this issue urge us to look backwards and forwards from the materials described above, and serve to emblematise the range and spread of Williams's influence into very different historical and cultural contexts. Olivia Smith, focusing on John Locke's plain style, demonstrates how important his time in rural Somerset in 1659 – away from the cities of London and Oxford – was for his intellectual development and commitment to the use of transparent, truthful language, which later became associated with the discourse of the Royal Society. The social agency of language is also the focus of the last essay in this issue, in which John Higgins explores the beginnings of changes to the institutional culture of contemporary South African university life – 'institutional culture as whiteness' – as the ratio of black to white students at historically white universities begins to shift. The issue concludes with a selection of reviews: Peter Marks discusses Hywel Dix's *After Raymond Williams: Cultural Materialism and the Breakup of Britain*; Gregory Woods reviews Stefania Michelucci's *The Poetry of Thom Gunn: A Critical Study*; Ben Harker assesses Jack Jones's 1935 novel *Black Parade*; and the selection closes with Sarah Davison's evaluation of *The Oxford Critical and Cultural History of Modernist Magazines. Volume 1. Britain and Ireland: 1880–1955*, jointly edited by the current chair of the Raymond Williams Society, Peter Brooker, and Andrew Thacker.

We are pleased to welcome new members to the Editorial Board: Simon Dentith and Ben Harker. Simon's work focuses on nineteenth-century writing, the work of William Morris, contemporary Scottish literature, and the historicity of writing; Ben, who guest-edited *Key Words* 7 on the 1930s and 40s, 'The Century's Wide Margin', also works on culture and the Left in Britain, on working-class writing, folk music, radical theatre and radio, and Marxist theories of culture. It is with much gratitude that we acknowledge the contribution of Claire Jowitt to *Key Words*; her energy and industry have invigorated the journal since its re-launch in 2007. Claire leaves the Editorial Board in order to take up a new challenge, to act as a General Editor of the new edition of Richard Hakluyt's *The Principal Navigations* (1598–1600) which OUP are publishing in fourteen volumes, and we wish her every success in this project. Special thanks are due to Jennifer Birkett for her valuable advice and support during the production of this issue.

We are still accepting submissions for *Key Words* 10 (2012) which will be a special issue devoted to a re-consideration, 50 years after its initial publication, of the ideas, significance and legacy of Raymond Williams's ground-breaking book *The Long Revolution* (1961). Articles for consideration should in the first instance be sent electronically to Catherine Clay at Catherine.clay@ntu.ac.uk

Editors' Preface

or in hard-copy to her at the School of Arts and Humanities, Nottingham Trent University, Clifton Campus, Nottingham NG11 8NS, United Kingdom, by 31 May 2011.

The journal is also pleased to announce that the Raymond Williams Society has launched a postgraduate student essay competition for work grounded in the tradition of cultural materialism. The aim is to encourage a new generation of scholars in this area, especially those who are engaged in discourses and approaches arising from the work of Raymond Williams. The prize for the winning entry is £100, and a year's subscription to the Society. The winning essay will also be considered for publication in a future issue of *Key Words*. Full details of the competition and terms of entry can be found at: http://www.raymondwilliams.co.uk/.

Notes

1   Raymond Williams, 'Culture is Ordinary', in *The Everyday Life Reader*, ed. Ben Highmore (London: Routledge, 2002), 95.

Retrieval and Beyond: Labouring-Class Writing
Tim Burke and John Goodridge

It is now 37 years since *The Country and the City* gave a significant role, in the dramatic narrative of the English representation of its spaces, to those who worked the land as well as to those who owned it or adopted a proprietorial gaze over it.[1] Nearly 30 years have passed since John Barrell first shone a torchlight on *The Dark Side of the Landscape* and David Vincent uncovered autobiographical riches in *Bread, Knowledge and Freedom*, and fully twenty since Donna Landry retrieved, from the remotest stacks of the British Library, a group of working women poets who have gone from being *The Muses of Resistance* to familiar figures in our conference halls and classrooms.[2] It is a good moment to take stock in the field of labouring-class cultural studies. Each of the contributions in the present volume can trace an origin somewhere in the discernible line of descent from Raymond Williams, but in the last two decades, the field has expanded rapidly and its lines of influence are ever more diffuse.

Since Landry's intervention, key events in the field have come at increasingly regular intervals. The nineties saw fuller critical integration of labouring-class cultural practitioners and practices. Student anthologies and critical studies alike testify to the altering environment, though the development was uneven. A flavour of the ambivalence that persisted in some quarters throughout the decade may be found in a review article that appeared in *Literature and History* in 2000.[3] 'Faces in the Crowd' begins with a wry comparison between the children's book *Where's Wally?*, in which the reader is taxed with finding Wally's face in a variety of crowd scenes that overwhelm the eye in their intricate detail, and the hunt for a canonical romantic poet in a sample of new monographs. Amidst the mediocrity and mendacity, the reviewer gladly happens upon a work of original scholarship rather than an exercise in retrieval – Anne Janowitz's *Lyric and Labour in the Romantic Tradition* (which remains the most substantial study of the past two decades)[4] – but the article's title betrays some of the critical anxieties persisting in that turn of the millennium moment. Suspicion and hostility have evaporated in the last decade. Online technologies and specialist anthologies have permitted widening access to labouring-class writings and the everyday worlds of lower-class Britons; dedicated academic centres have emerged (and other developments include the appointment of one of the present editors to a dedicated Research Fellowship in Labouring-Class Writing). Unmined sources have been tapped, revealing for example a covert underground radical theatre scene in Georgian London which provided opportunities for plebeian dramatists and performers alike, or the full contributions of labouring participants in nineteenth-century radical politics and journalism. Working-class fiction is attracting new attention (thanks in some measure to a special issue of *Key Words* in 2007: Issue 5, 'Working Spaces, Working Lives'); the religious activities and writings of workers is a nascent but important sub-field; the peculiar figure of the working-class intellectual is the subject of an important new collection of essays; the understanding of the labourer as reader has been advanced immeasurably by Jonathan Rose's *The Intellectual Life of the Working Classes,* a study which, together with William St Clair's *The Reading Nation in the Romantic Period,* has made the discipline of book history seem vital again.[5] With Yale University Press preparing a tenth anniversary edition of Rose's *Intellectual Life*, the author reflects in this issue on the remarkable uptake of its innovative methodology, and accounts for its lasting impact.

The principal focus of this issue remains, however, on labouring-class writers, and the pre-eminent discipline remains poetry. John Clare's ascent continues: he is now the subject of several major biographies and critical studies, with more in the pipeline, though the stronger indication of his cultural mainstreaming is perhaps his presence on the English GCSE examination syllabus. In Wales, the reputation of the controversial stonemason-bard Iolo Morganwg has never been higher, thanks to a dedicated series of monographs, editions and selections from his writings. In Scottish studies, James Hogg's diverse body of literary and musical work is being edited with scholarly thoroughness, though Robert Burns remains the central figure. The 250th anniversary of the bard has been celebrated with a number of major studies of both the life and the works, after several comparatively lean years in Burns scholarship. Among the more surprising developments in the field of poetry has been a remarkable rise in the significance of Robert Bloomfield. Notwithstanding his status as a best-selling poet and (in the view of Coleridge) a major presence in the contemporary poetic scene, throughout the twentieth century the Suffolk farm worker turned London shoemaker occupied a particularly dark place in the critical landscape: condemned to skulk in the shadow of John Clare, as Clare himself was once placed in Wordsworth's shadow. Ironically, Williams played a significant part in the diminution of Bloomfield, elevating Clare's tragic stature to such an extent in *The Country and the City* that Bloomfield's work was made to seem low, even comically trivial by comparison. Alongside Clare, boldly initiating new structures of feeling in the form of his 'green language' and readily recruitable to the dialectical trajectory of Williams's historical narrative, Bloomfield was portrayed as absurdly servile in his seeming support of the existing poetic and social orders.

While Clare challenged the enclosure acts as deleterious to both nature and poetry, Bloomfield's efforts to ground poetry in rural realities are, Williams finds, themselves 'enclosed within a kind of external pointing and explanation' that locates his verse outside and above the realities it sought to represent, though always comfortably within conventional pastoral structures. Worse, his 'creeping humility is an acquired taste', though 'if it now provokes anger or contempt we must not make the mistake of attacking Bloomfield but the men, the class, who reduced him and many thousands of others to this obeisance'.[6] Styled in this way, it is hardly surprising that Clare's life becomes 'more tragic but also more urgent: more tragic because more urgent';[7] the distinction, already secure, held for another 30 years after *The Country and the City* appeared. But both McEathron in this issue, and Tim Fulford and Lynda Pratt, in the newly available edition of Bloomfield's correspondence, identify a potentially limiting romantic tendency in such categories. We are now not so interested in Bloomfield the man or how the work was shaped by the life, perhaps, so much as what his success suggests about romantic reading cultures, or the changing patterns of patronage, or the historical sidelining of the georgic model of ecology he represented in favour of lyric individuation and yet more pastoral romanticisations of the author and the nature of the literary work he performs. William St Clair's 2004 study of romantic-period reading habits provides a model of literary significance that in statistical terms alone makes the case for Bloomfield's reintegration into the period's poetic constellations; the critical work of Simon White, Roger Sales, John Lucas, and among many others, McEathron himself, continues to detect in Bloomfield the political and poetical sophistications that in the 1970s were being attributed exclusively to Clare.

Amongst these are a green 'agenda' that is both less explicit and extensive than Clare's, but significant nonetheless. A de-romanticised ecological aesthetic has been located in Bloomfield both by Bridget Keegan, in her 2008 study of *British Labouring-Class Nature Writing, 1730–1837*, and by Donna Landry in her essay, 'Georgic Ecology'.[8] In her present piece Landry develops the premise of that article, extending it to a consideration of the emergent field of animal studies, and the connections with labouring-class studies that such enquiries imply. The scholarship of animal studies has enjoyed a spectacular rise to prominence via the interventions of Donna Haraway, Jacques Derrida and Landry herself. Animals and animal scholarship are analogous to the labouring classes and to labouring-class studies, in so far as they experience the subaltern difficulty of self-representation and the hazards of being represented from 'without'. The analogy is revealed as of long standing (pre-dating Marx's analogies by at least a century) in Landry's provocative contribution, which both documents the work done to date and proposes that animals need a history and historians 'devoted to representing their interests'.

Among the literary historians devoted to just such a representation is Anne Milne. Her 2008 monograph, *Lactilla Tends Her Fav'rite Cow: Ecocritical*

Tim Burke and John Goodridge

Readings of Women and Animals in Eighteenth-Century British Laboring-Class Poetry, reveals that in the later eighteenth century, women writers, especially those from the ranks of the labouring poor, are especially attuned to the inequities of human culture and in human–animal interactions.[9] In Milne's contribution to this issue, she provides a pertinent restatement of the value of ecocriticism in cultural materialist practice. She finds in Raymond Williams's diachronic etymologies an early sensitivity to the distinction between classical realist models of space as 'settings' privileging those human interactions which occur in them, and a more sensitive and historicised notion of 'place'. As in her book, labouring writers are here viewed, via the nature of their work and the cultural traditions arising in work, as more acutely sensitised to the ontological possibilities of a land conceived as more than property or setting.

A long neglected male writer with a sophisticated sense of self, place and environment, the Scottish poet and ornithologist Alexander Wilson, is the subject of Bridget Keegan's contribution to this issue. Keegan's recent monograph quietly suggested the need for a radical shake-up in ways of conceptualising the labouring-class poetic tradition. Increasingly marooned in studies of individual authors and their inevitably remarkable biographies, some recent scholarship has come close to inadvertently replicating aspects of the very romantic faith in the exceptional genius which it purports to critique. Keegan, though, has found new ways of envisioning the tradition, organising it not by author but by environmental factors, occupational interests, and religious beliefs. While in this essay she focuses on an individual author, the principal objective of her reading of his verse is wider. She demonstrates how an emigrant author of labouring-class origins helped to shape a specifically American sense of landscape and wilderness that depended upon the removal from the scene of a native American presence. Wilson's own alien status in this space complicates his position: his 'freedom to roam and to hunt is simultaneously an appropriation of bourgeois and upper-class British modes of engaging the environment, but also emulates, in other ways, Native American practices of being in nature, even as it signals the disappearance and dispossession of the Indians'. Keegan convincingly makes the case not just for Wilson but for further study of other transatlantic romantic-period writings by labouring authors, and reminds us too that our knowledge of plebeian British emigrant authors remains significantly under-developed.

Two further essays deal with another under-developed area of enquiry in labouring-class poetry studies, namely genre. Contemporary critics minded to find fault with labouring poets in the eighteenth and nineteenth centuries often seized upon the poets' generic choices as evidence of an imitative rather than an original imagination. William J. Christmas's contention in these pages is that we need to remain attentive to the ways in which labouring-class writers subvert, adapt and reconfigure the styles and modes available to them from what was often, inevitably, a limited exposure to models of poetic expression. The most easily available model was not, of course, Thomson, nor indeed Milton, Shakespeare or Virgil, but the Bible, and yet the rich and diverse body of religious writing by labourers remains largely untouched by modern scholarship. This tells us much more about our own concerns and priorities than it does of the historical periods and figures we study, but Christmas is amongst those who are undertaking the retrieval of a long neglected corpus of works. In his essay here, he finds that religious and gendered discourse is productively combined: Mary Masters, for example, after being '[d]iscouraged from the classical tradition by her father … turned to the Bible for poetic inspiration and raw material'. But her periphrastic verses are neither simple acquiescing in patriarchal expectations of proper femininity, nor simple translations: Christmas suggests that verse like this requires us to be alert to evidence of 'generic hybridisation that signals to the reader a greater latitude with regard to topical content and, hence, potential meaning beyond the merely religious or devotional'; specifically, Masters can subtly fuse conventional paraphrase with the eighteenth-century verse epistle, effectively converting a psalm about masculine retribution into a feminist complaint about the wrongs done by men to her sex.

In addition to surveying the vast array of similar hybridisations in nineteenth-century labouring women's poetry, Florence Boos detects several generic innovations. The 'ballad of memorie' is perhaps the most significant of these. It connects traditional oral culture, with which many such poets remained familiar, either through their rural background or the nature of their occupations, with a sense of the need to record authentically the experience of the working woman, memories which could not be transmitted adequately through the many fictional working women – Peggoty, Nelly Dean, the Seamstress Miriam in *Aurora Leigh*, et al. – who appear in the novels and narrative poems of middle-class authors. Such ballads demonstrate their authors' 'ardent desire to add a corrective truth – a dissenting "memorie"– to more familiar canonical representations of literary consciousness'.

Finally, two essays in this special issue take us beyond the concern with poetic expression to focus on aspects of labouring-class cultural production and consumption that have not been accorded the attention they deserve: literary criticism, and the visual arts.

Brian Maidment makes a powerful call for greater attention to be paid to the many branches of popular visual art in the early nineteenth century. The study of early Victorian graphic satire, he contends, has been largely shaped by Fredric Jameson, and by Allon White and Peter Stallybrass in their study of *The Politics and Poetics of Transgression*:[10] their arguments that images of urban working people are principally to do with the development and cathartic processing of middle-class ideology have effectively held sway for over two decades. Such arguments remain valid and useful, Maidment suggests; but forgotten in the attention paid to commodification and the repression of social anxiety was any possibility that such comic visual art can also be understood as 'forming a representational site through which detailed understanding of the nature of the labouring class experience might be undertaken'. In his essay here, Maidment makes a compelling case for the new view that will obtain when the graphic technologies and the new methods of representation they enabled are fully historicised and the many subgenres of visual art are more carefully distinguished. He makes it clear that such a project is only just underway, and concedes too that plebeian contributors to the visual art tradition are frustratingly few in number; but he also predicts, with justified confidence, that being able to read the rise of 'comic naturalism', made possible by the contemporary developments in wood engraving, will produce a corresponding knowledge of how the 'comic art of the 1820s, 1830s and 1840s' could become 'so suggestive a medium for the study of the street presence and the domestic life of the urban lower orders'.

We have become accustomed to thinking of labouring-class authors as the subjects of literary criticism, but Michael Sanders' essay suggests that critical studies of the British literary tradition, some of it penned by plebeian authors, were widely available in the proletarian press in the 1830s and 1840s. Building on the early researches in this field by Paul Murphy, and its more substantial treatment in Anne Janowitz's *Lyric and Labour*, Sanders reveals more of the extent, the diversity, and the subtlety of the criticism published in this period. The pages of the Scottish *Chartist Circular*, for example, host debates on whether poetry is an instrument of liberation or oppression, the work of Byron, Scott and Burns generating particularly fierce defences and attacks, though always in its pages, a faith in 'the close association between emotional affect and political effect remains a constant'.

Our own study of poetry and other acts of cultural creation and consumption has only recently begun to move significantly beyond these related concerns. Since Williams helped to reintroduce us to Duck and Clare some 40 years ago, we have tended to be inspired by the emotional effectiveness and/or the political efficacy of such cultural practices amongst the labouring artists we have helped to retrieve. The essays in this special issue, demanding our attention to new areas of study and new ways of reinterpreting familiar material without prioritising authorial biography, mark another milestone in our long revolution of literary criticism.

To provide an up-to-date snapshot of current labouring-class studies, we have commissioned five 'think pieces' and interspersed them among the five more substantial essays included in this special number. We discuss these short comments along with the essays, above, but it is worth summarising their content here. Two of them focus on key individuals: David Fairer makes critically perceptive remarks on the Bristol poet Ann Yearsley (*c*.1753–1806), routinely diminished for the last two centuries under the soubriquet of 'the milkmaid poet' but finally emerging in the critical arena as the serious philosophical poet she courageously aspired to be; while Scott McEathron offers a thoughtful account of the once-famous Robert Bloomfield (1766–1823), John Clare's 'English Theocritus', who is now re-emerging into the light through a series of recent scholarly projects, notably the Romantic Circles online edition of his voluminous and absorbing correspondence. Two other pieces, by Donna Landry and Anne Milne, situate labouring-class studies in terms of the sister fields of animal studies and ecocriticism, a welcome move towards finding appropriate theoretical positionings for this emerging field of study. Finally, Jonathan Rose looks back on his keynote study, *The Intellectual Life of the British Working Classes*, and forward through current and possible future approaches to the field, centring finally on the important if contested term 'middlebrow'.

Notes
1 Raymond Williams, *The Country and The City* (London: Chatto and Windus, 1973).
2 John Barrell, *The Dark Side of the Landscape: The Rural Poor in English Painting, 1730–1840* (Cambridge: Cambridge University Press, 1980); David Vincent, *Bread, Knowledge and Freedom: a Study of Nineteenth-Century Working Class Autobiography* (London and New York: Methuen, 1981); Donna Landry, *The Muses of Resistance: Laboring-Class Women's Poetry in Britain, 1739–1796* (Cambridge: Cambridge University Press, 1990).
3 Robin Jarvis, 'Faces in the Crowd: Directions in Romantic Studies', *Literature & History* 9, no. 2 (Autumn 2000), 69–76.
4 Anne Janowitz, *Lyric and Labour in the Romantic Tradition* (Cambridge: Cambridge University Press, 1998).
5 Aruna Krishamurthy (ed.), *The Working-Class Intellectual in Eighteenth- and Nineteenth-Century Britain* (Farnham: Ashgate, 2009); Jonathan Rose, *The Intellectual Life of the British Working Classes* (New Haven, CT: Yale University Press, 2001); William St Clair, *The Reading Nation in the Romantic Period* (Cambridge: Cambridge University Press, 2004).
6 Williams, *The Country and the City*, 134.
7 Williams, *The Country and the City*, 136.
8 Bridget Keegan, *British Labouring-Class Nature Writing, 1730–1837* (Houndmills and New York: Palgrave Macmillan, 2008); Donna Landry, 'Georgic Ecology', in *Robert Bloomfield: Lyric, Class and the Romantic Canon*, ed. Simon White, John Goodridge, and Bridget Keegan (Lewisburg, PA: Bucknell University Press, 2006).
9 Anne Milne, *'Lactilla Tends her Fav'rite Cow': Ecocritical Readings of Animals and Women in Eighteenth-Century British Labouring-Class Women's Poetry* (Lewisburg, PA: Bucknell University Press, 2008).
10 Allon White and Peter Stallybrass, *The Politics and Poetics of Transgression* (London: Methuen, 1986).

Brute Strength: Labouring-Class Studies and Animal Studies
Donna Landry

Any new constituency enters the terrain of scholarship ineluctably shadowed by the first such constituency, the working class. In the case of animals, or, more precisely, non-human animals, a relationship to human labourers casts a particularly long shadow.

'They cannot represent themselves, they must be represented', Marx wrote of the French peasants who did not perceive themselves to form a class but remained marooned in their singularity. Divided into separate families and households, they no more constituted a self-conscious collectivity, Marx added, than a sack of potatoes constitutes a self-conscious collectivity. It was therefore not surprising, although regrettable, Marx concluded in *The Eighteenth Brumaire of Louis Bonaparte*, that the peasantry embraced being represented symbolically by Napoleon, despite the fact that he could in no sense be said to be acting in their interests.[1]

Animal collectivities do not clamour for political representation or identify symbolically with human or other political leaders, so far as we know. Animal claims to identity politics within the academy are the product of human social movements rather than non-human animal ones. Animals do not speak to us of their right to representation, or, if they do speak to us in these terms, we are incapable of hearing them. In this sense, animals constitute a subaltern group. As Gayatri Chakravorty Spivak has endeavoured to clarify in recent years, her famous contention that 'the subaltern cannot speak' was situated within an understanding of speech-act theory. As she puts it in an interview, it was not that the subaltern could not literally speak or talk but that even when the subaltern made an effort unto the death to speak, the forces of hegemony could not hear, and the speech-act was not complete.[2]

How much more dense is the silence of the animal subaltern, then, giving rise to innumerable speculations by philosophers about what it would mean if animals could talk, and if they could, whether we would understand them, and what that might in turn signify.

Both constituencies, labouring on behalf of the human elite, became politically discernible, though not yet subject to political representation, during the eighteenth century. There seems to be a certain affinity between scholarly work on the labouring masses, and on animals and the natural world, just as there persists a certain affinity between feminist work and work on animals.[3]

Discourses of the dignity of labour were largely coterminous with discourses of sympathy for the brute creation from the mid-eighteenth century onwards. We can see this secret concatenation, as Samuel Johnson might have put it, first occurring during the early 1750s, when Thomas Gray composed his *Elegy Written in a Country Church-yard* – memorialising the unrepresented labouring poor – and John Hawkesworth published *Adventurer* number 37 – comparing the lives of a donkey and a horse as class-specific varieties of cruelty; the horse's experience of high life and fall into misery over and against the donkey's low-born life of continual suffering.[4]

As I have argued in *Noble Brutes*, the peculiarities of the equid make him especially comparable with human labourers, particularly during horse-powered eras.[5] Like the human labourer, the horse is subject to ennobling improvement, on the one hand, and to casual brutality, on the other. This complicity of relationship is now being reproduced within academic scholarship. The new Animal Studies within humanities disciplines seeks to represent non-human animals as potentially both subjects and agents of history.[6] Like the labouring classes before them, animals now emerge as silenced masses in need of spokespeople, or at least historians devoted to representing their interests.

Notes

1 Karl Marx, *The Eighteenth Brumaire of Louis Bonaparte*, in *Surveys from Exile*, ed. David Fernbach (New York: Vintage Books, 1974).
2 Gayatri Chakravorty Spivak, 'Can the Subaltern Speak?', in *Marxism and the Interpretation of Culture*, ed. Cary Nelson and Lawrence Grossberg (Urbana: University of Illinois Press, 1988), 271–313; and 'Subaltern Talk: Interview with the Editors', in *The Spivak Reader*, ed. Donna Landry and Gerald MacLean (New York and London: Routledge, 1996), 287–308.
3 See, for example, Bridget Keegan, *British Labouring-Class Nature Writing, 1730–1837* (Houndmills and New York: Palgrave Macmillan, 2008); Anne Milne, *'Lactilla Tends her Fav'rite Cow': Ecocritical Readings of Animals and Women in Eighteenth-Century British Labouring-Class Women's Poetry* (Lewisburg, PA: Bucknell University Press, 2008).
4 John Hawkesworth, *The Adventurer*, no. 37, Tuesday, 13 March 1753, 217–22.
5 Donna Landry, *Noble Brutes: How Eastern Horses Transformed English Culture* (Baltimore, MD and London: The Johns Hopkins University Press, 2008).
6 See, for example, The Animal Studies Group, *Killing Animals* (Urbana and Chicago: University of Illinois Press, 2006); Marianne DeKoven, 'Guest Column: Why Animals Now?', and contributions by many hands to 'Theories and Methodologies: Animal Studies', in *PMLA: Publications of the Modern Language Association of America* 124, no. 2 (March 2009), 361–69 and 472–575; Jacques Derrida, 'The Animal that Therefore I Am (More to Follow)', trans. David Wills,

Critical Inquiry 28, no. 2 (Winter 2002), 369–418; Jacques Derrida, 'And Say the Animal Responded?', trans. David Wills, in *Zoontologies: The Question of the Animal*, ed. Cary Wolfe (Minneapolis and London: University of Minnesota Press, 2003), 121–46; Erica Fudge, *Brutal Reasoning: Animals, Rationality, and Humanity in Early Modern England* (Ithaca, NY and London: Cornell University Press, 2006); Donna J. Haraway, *When Species Meet* (Minneapolis and London: University of Minnesota Press, 2008); Donna J. Haraway, *The Companion Species Manifesto: Dogs, People, and Significant Otherness* (Chicago: Prickly Paradigm Press, 2003); Cary Wolfe, *Animal Rites: American Culture, the Discourse of Species, and Posthumanist Theory* (Chicago and London: University of Chicago Press, 2003).

Close Reading Yearsley
David Fairer

The phenomenal expansion of the canon of eighteenth-century poetry during the past twenty years has allowed many new voices to be heard, and among the recoveries none has proved so striking and refreshing as those of labouring-class women poets. Mary Collier, Mary Leapor, and Ann Yearsley in particular have been welcomed onto university English courses, and students are fascinated by what they have to say, not least by the situations, topics and experiences about which they speak. They represent, in part, an unofficial, 'authentic' eighteenth century in which real people led genuine lives outside the sanctioned confines of culture. Their poetry too seems to break away from conventional generic models: in *The Woman's Labour* (1739), 'Crumble-Hall' (1751), and 'Clifton Hill' (1785), the georgic poem, the estate poem, and the prospect poem all gain a new dimension. To date, the challenge has been to find ways of bringing these women into the story, whether speaking from 'outside' as writers excluded from the canon, or, more subtly, as poets whose work can be integrated into the literary history of the period, and in that way help to re-shape it. The latter is perhaps the harder task, but the one that does these women better service.

It may be, however, that we still haven't attended closely enough to the individual voices of labouring-class women poets. It is as if we are still not wholly convinced they can stand up for themselves, and that they are only fully empowered as labouring-class women rather than simply as poets. A lot of valuable scholarly and critical work has been done in mapping out critical and socio-historical contexts for their work, and poets like Collier, Leapor and Yearsley have found a significance and a strength that has made them absolutely necessary for those of us who admire them. They are now an integral part of the literary scene. As a result the landscape of eighteenth-century poetry has changed – at least it has for those critics prepared to engage with their work within the bigger picture of literary history. But this representativeness is where a potential limitation arises. It is easy (unknowingly) to patronise them by treating them as interesting phenomena, case studies of poets who successfully struggled to find a voice within a canon still dominated by the major male writers. Their work undoubtedly has a representative or exemplary value; but they tend to speak more powerfully as labouring-class women rather than as poets in their own right with specific concerns and individual ideas. To analyse their poetic language in detail might be thought to limit them by narrowing the focus and ignoring their wider significance. Understandably we want to view them within their own world, and not force them into a more traditional critical context and value-system that might reinforce the idea that they are simply 'minor' but 'interesting'. But that 'world', rather than wholly liberating, can itself become a restriction, a defensive move. The thought arises that we may be avoiding close textual analysis because in our heart of hearts we are unsure whether they can withstand scrutiny.

Ann Yearsley's poem 'The Fragment', for example, which was printed in her first subscription volume of 1785, offers itself to us as a poem that confronts the problem of being articulate and locating a receptive audience. We have only to quote lines 14–22 to hear her voicing the predicament of someone for whom the very act of speaking out is fraught with difficulty:

> Yet, yet indulge not, list'ning winds may catch
> Coherent sighs, and waft them far away,
> Where levity holds high the senseless roar
> Of laughter, and pale woe, abash'd, retires.
> Or, shou'd my woes be to the winds diffus'd,
> No longer mine, once past the quiv'ring lip;
> Like flying atoms in the sightless air,
> Some might descend on the gay, grinning herd;
> But few, how few, wou'd reach the feeling mind![1]

Given such a scenario, communication is virtually impossible. We can quote the phrase 'no longer mine' and note the irony that the Bristol milkwoman will soon feel the full force of the idea that her poems are no longer hers, edited, packaged, introduced, and finally appropriated, by her over-zealous patroness. The problem of speaking out and the problem of ownership are brought together in the most striking way. In this reading, Yearsley's situation seems to strengthen the poem. But as we offer this entirely valid and interesting reading we may be missing a further dimension of Yearsley's language. Our picture of Yearsley the Bristol milkwoman may be distracting us from Yearsley the philosophically minded, sceptical enquirer, a poet who is less concerned with her own situation than with the intellectual problem of speech itself. Up to this point in the poem she has been running the predictable sentimental gamut of sighs, groans, and tears ('here heave, my heart, / Here sigh thy woes away; unheard the groan, / Unseen the falling tear', lines 9–11), which makes her sudden self-admonishment ('Yet, yet indulge not') all the more striking and deserving of attention. To that point she has had no difficulty in finding her voice: the predictability of the language tells us that if she wished to continue in that vein she would have audience enough. The significance of lines 14–22 is that she is at this point in the poem stopping herself from being too easily fluent. She is checking her obvious facility in handling the expected emotional expressions, and now complicates and questions the kind of poem her readers may be expecting. It would have been all too easy for her to speak as an unlearned, unsophisticated 'voice of nature' here. But instead she becomes awkward and checks her reader as well. Rather than continue the expressive plaint, she jolts us by letting her words slip away, and as she does so she consciously moves from coherence to dispersal. The 'quiv'ring lip' is no longer the mark of an authentic sensibility but becomes the crucial boundary between thought and speech, the point where expression occurs, where the thought has to fend for itself. We are made to think about the nature of 'coherent' meaning in the poem – indeed how expression and coherence can be reconciled in any poem, not just hers. The 'flying atoms in the sightless air' are not just a mark of her individual dilemma, or of her position as a labouring-class woman writer struggling for expression, but rather of her philosophical curiosity. There are complex layers of possibility here, which she is struggling to express, but such a 'struggle' is an intellectual one. She is pushing the idea further than other poets. She wonders about the relation between emotion and speech, about the problems of subjective experience, and how the receptive audience may assemble those 'flying atoms' as they themselves choose. The 'atoms' may pour down on the mindless many, possibly wasted but also potentially satiric too; or they may work their way more precariously into a few thoughtful and responsive readers – the phrase 'reach the feeling heart' was clearly the predictable wording readily at hand, but Yearsley's intelligence, her awareness of the problem she wrestles with, leads her to the less obvious phrase, 'feeling mind'. It is the enigmatic relationship between *feeling* and *mind* that has set her on the trail in this passage, pursuing the thought from line to line, at the risk of being herself awkward and incoherent, in order to track the idea. There is an exploratory intensity here that we can miss if we limit Yearsley to voicing a representative predicament rather than raising questions about how sensibility negotiates between subjectivities.

Note

[1] *Poems, on Several Occasions. By Ann Yearsley, A Milkwoman of Bristol* (London: T. Cadell, 1785), 38. The poem is included in *Ann Yearsley: Selected Poems*, ed. Tim Burke (Cheltenham: The Cyder Press, 2003), 1–3.

Not So Lowly Bards: Working-Class Women Poets and Middle-Class Expectations
Florence Boos

There are several reasons for the neglect of working-class Victorian women's poetry. One – the most salient, perhaps – is that working-class literature has traditionally been identified with Chartist and dialect poetry.[1] Another surely lies in the biased historical record: verses which working- and middle-class editors dismissed as insignificant are unlikely to emerge unscathed a century and a half later. A third, however, may be found in the heterogeneity of what little has survived, which ranged from the verses by scarcely literate authors to sophisticated works by women deeply influenced and informed by prior literary traditions. Working-class women were strongly imprinted by their regions, occupations and degrees of access to education, perhaps to an even greater degree than more conventionally educated poets, so that it is difficult to frame valid general interpretations of their poetry.

Mindful of these personal and regional qualities, I have tried to reconstruct in some detail the concrete historical and biographical contexts of the seventeen authors I introduced in *Women Poets of Victorian Britain: An Anthology*.[2] In the present essay I will give greater attention to contrasts and divergences between working-class women and their middle- and upper-class counterparts – in subject-matter primarily, but also in nuances of tone, emphasis, language and generic choice.

More precisely, I will focus on

1 contemporary representations of violence against women and portrayals of sexuality and 'fallen' women;
2 preferences for ballads and songs over more 'formal' genres such as blank verse and the dramatic monologue; and
3 direct autobiographical expressions and appeals to regional and 'people's history'.

A preoccupation with domestic violence was evident in the works of writers from several regions, and almost all working-class women writers shunned poetic homages to the 'field of honor'.[3] A disproportionate number of the poets whose works have survived were Scottish,[4] and several of them – inspired in part by ballad traditions, and encouraged by the universally admired work of Burns – wrote 'people's-historical' accounts of the 'Clearances' and other events which disrupted the lives of ordinary people.

All the working-class women poets I have found naturally sought to grace their work with metaphors and comparisons derived from their reading. But few of them had access to the classical education displayed by middle-class poets such as Elizabeth Barrett Browning, Augusta Webster, Emily Pfeiffer or Michael Field, and most evoked contemporary events and more direct personal experiences in their works.

Sexuality and Domestic Violence

Middle- and upper-class women wrote sympathetic portrayals of 'fallen' middle-class women who violated Victorian sexual norms, and focused on the shame, isolation and emotional betrayal they suffered, as well as the 'genteel' double standards they confronted in their everyday lives.[5] Working-class women poets wrote more directly and forcefully about drunkenness, domestic abuse and sexual violence – rare subjects in the works of middle-class women poets with the exception of Barrett Browning's *Aurora Leigh* and 'The Runaway Slave at Pilgrim's Point'.[6] They were also more likely to suggest that 'fallenness' was a matter of economic survival, and treat desertion, single motherhood and exchanges of sex for money as recurrent aspects of working-class life.

Fanny Forrester (1852–89), for example, a Salford factory worker, expressed explicit sympathy with streetwalkers, whom she considered victims of the immiseration of the rural poor, and her middle-class editor Ben Brierley felt called upon to defend her 'respectability' as follows: 'Miss Forrester is neither vulgar nor unladylike … [It is wrong to assume that] because a poor girl works at a mill she must, of necessity, be deficient in those qualities that are supposed to adorn her wealthier sisters.'[7]

The 'factory girl' Ellen Johnston was a rare working-class woman writer who expressed poetic desire in erotic rather than sentimental terms, and who may have been the only Victorian poet who acknowledged her motherhood of an illegitimate child. In the first edition of her *Autobiography, Poems and Songs*, she addressed 'A Mother's Love' to the child she 'first did behold in sorrow and sin / Thou sweet offspring of false love – my Mary Achin' – and remarked in the volume's introduction that she

> could no longer conceal what the world falsely calls a woman's shame … I never loved life more dearly and longed for the hour when I would have something to love me.[8]

Johnston's daughter Mary (Achinvole) Johnston survived to offer a home to Johnston in her final illness, but the forthright remarks just quoted disappeared in the volume's second edition.[9] Johnston was also rare in her willingness to write first-person expressions of erotic love, as when she confessed to the unidentified subject of 'The Happy Man':

> 'Tis not alone by light of day that I do think of thee,
> For in the lonely midnight hour still thou art there with me!
> And the dreams of sweet delusion that wander through my brain –
> They waken me to madness that words can never name.[10]

Janet Hamilton (1795–1873), married at 13 and the mother of seven surviving children, devoted several poems to the subject of desertion. The most striking may have been 'A Ballad o' Mary Muiren', in which she described the desertion and death of the daughter of 'a friend'. Her lifelong friend and patron Alexander Wallace later reported that Hamilton's family was deeply moved when her daughter 'Mirren' (Marion), who lived with her mother and cared for her in her final illness, read aloud from one of Hamilton's other expressions of poetic sympathy for a deserted woman.[11]

Working-class women poets' representations of violence also differed from those of their working-class male counterparts in their focus on domestic rather than political conflicts. Chartists and other working-class male poets of the period often denounced acts of economic violence as marks of capitalist greed, and condoned political violence as acts of retaliation and/or class resistance. W.J. Linton's 1851 'Revenge', for example, portrayed the murder of a callous landlord, and Gerald Massey's 'A Red Republican Lyric' and 'Son of the Red Republican' enjoined the murder of tyrants, as did passages from Thomas Cooper's 'The Purgatory of Suicides' and Ernest Jones's 'The Song of the Low' ('The thrust of a poor man's arm will go / Through the heart of the proudest king!').[12]

Working-class women, by contrast – with the rare exception of Ruth Wills in 'Zenobia', a poem in which a black slave kills her cruel mistress – tended to represent instances of violence as brutal but commonplace acts of everyday cruelty – men against wives, parents against children, and children against aged parents. And in their temperance verse – a now disregarded poetic subgenre at which almost every working-class woman poet tried her hand – they associated such everyday violence with drunken rage.

In 'The Drunkard's Inhumanity' in *Homely Rhymes from the Banks of the Jed* (1887), for example, Agnes Mabon, an invalided factory worker, confronted readers with a wife's body 'rendered … [o]ne dark discoloured mass of aching flesh' and focused on '… [the] pang that rends the bleeding heart. / The disappointed love, the shame, the grief …'.[13]

Janet Hamilton associated alcoholism with domestic violence, and may have been best known to her contemporaries as a 'temperance poet'. In 'Oor Location', for example, her bitterly sardonic description of changes her village had suffered during her lifetime, she took the time to rage evenhandedly against poverty and rotgut:

> An' noo I'm fairly set a-gaun,
> On baith the whisky-shop and pawn;
> I'll speak my min' – and what for no?
> Frae whence cums misery, want an' wo,
> The ruin, crime, disgrace, an' shame,
> That quenches a' the lichts o' hame,
> Ye needna speer, the feck ot's drawn
> Out o' the change-hoose and the pawn […][14]

In 'The Contrast', a man

> … waits for [his wife's] returning,
> Wrath and hate within him burning […]
> Blows and shrieks and curses mingle –
> Words of passion, fierce and wild.[15]

In her essay 'Intemperance vs. the Moral Law', Hamilton described in direct, personal terms an alcoholic son who had threatened to kill his parents if they denied him what he wanted.

> We have known, ay, and seen – alas! that we should say so; it was not a solitary instance – a grey-haired mother, on her own hearth, shrinking from the presence of her own son, who, with murderous threats, uplifted hand, and eyes flaming with patricidal fires, was demanding from her the means to procure further indulgence in his depraved and brutal tastes. We have seen a father, day after day, forgetting to eat his bread, and nightly steeping his couch with tears, for the dishonour and apparent perdition of his son ….[16]

In another passage, she recalled:

> A youth of seventeen [who] became a confirmed drunkard … He is now nearly fifty years of age… He has … during all this time … gone half-naked and almost wholly barefoot … But it is not the appearance of the outward man, however shocking – it is the sad condition of the wretch's mind that we deplore. It is so utterly devoid of all feeling that he daily extorts his

food from the hands of his aged and invalid parents, who have nothing to spare ... but they have to choose between giving way to his demands, or, by refusing them, be overwhelmed by a torrent of outrageous threats and shocking blasphemies.[17]

It is possible that these impassioned memories were autobiographical; Hamilton's oldest son, a 30-year-old shoemaker in the 1841 census, would have been 51 or 52 when her essay appeared in 1863.[18]

In the last quarter of the century – partly, perhaps, in the wake of a Parliamentary Report on wife-beating and wife-murder which appeared in 1875 – working-class women and middle-class reformers such as Frances Power Cobbe began to uncouple acts of domestic violence from the alleged excuse of drunken rage.[19] In 'Women's Rights vs. Women's Wrongs', for example, one of the poems in her 1877 *The Blinkin' o' the Fire*, the former seamstress Jessie Russell (1850–1923) expressed solidarity with 'many a drudge to be found / In our city gentlemen's houses, in those kitchens underground', but offered her most heartfelt compassion for

> ... many a one [who] bears a greater wrong[,] who is called by the name of wife,
> While the dogs which follow her brutal lord lead not such a wretched life;
> But a life for a life, and the murderer's hung, and we think not the law inhuman,
> Then why not the lash for the man who kicks or strikes a defenceless woman?[20]

Working-class women poets, in brief, confronted sexual violence more directly and more often than their middle-class sisters. Earlier in the Victorian period, they channelled their opposition quite naturally into denunciations of alcoholic violence.[21] As the century waned, they and their middle-class allies shifted from a primary focus on alcoholism, and began to explore the underlying social and sexual psychology of a social order in which a man's wife and children were his 'possessions'. Along the way, their sublimated protests began to undercut Victorian truisms about the sanctity of family life, and exposed the complex wefts of violence and respectability that permeated its class hierarchies.

Poetic Forms and Craft

Another divide which separated working-class poets and memoirists from their more genteel sisters lay along different fault lines. Working-class women poets identified in different ways with the formal and generic traditions of their craft – in part, of course, because of their more limited access to formal education, but in part because they made much more direct and immediate use of the oral, regional and denominational 'demotic' traditions in which they were raised.

Consider, for example, the genre of the 'dramatic monologue'. Elizabeth Barrett Browning and other middle-class writers[22] employed it to evoke sympathy for outcasts whom 'respectable' readers might condemn out of hand – a rape victim about to be stoned to death for infanticide, for example. Working-class women poets needed no such shocks of recognition to identify with the 'lower orders' – in varying degrees they *were* the lower orders.

Ellen Johnston's denunciation of the 'funny warld' in 'A Last Sark', presented in the voice of a starving mother, may be the best-known miniature example of the genre:

> … for it's no divided fair,
> And whiles I think some o' the rich have got the puir folk's share,
> Tae see us starving here the nicht wi' no ae bless'd bawbee –
> What care some gentry if they're weel though a' the puir wad dee![23]

Less well-known monologues included Johnston's 'Come Awa' Jamie', in which a factory worker toils in inadequate light;[24] Fanny Forrester's 'The Bitter Task', in which a jilted unwed mother confesses to her son that she must sew the bridal dress for his father's wealthy new bride; Forrester's 'In the Workhouse – A Deserter's Story', in which a disgraced dying man decried a life of class-driven injustice;[25] and 'The Prison Cell', by Elizabeth Campbell (1804–1878), which explored the shame and abasement of a falsely accused man thrown into jail:

> My head ached, I fainted and fell,
> When they lock'd me up in a prison cell.
>
> And perjurers swearing away my good name,
> That shock pass'd away like a horrible dream.
> And with it the lightness of my youthful mind,
> And sad was the sorrow that brooded behind.[26]

Working-class women – especially those fortunate enough to benefit from the worker's education movement – also wrote from time to time in more elaborate formal genres. In 'Lament Written On the Death of the Rev. George Legge', for example, Ruth Wills composed a formal ode after the manner of 'Ode: Intimations of Immorality.'[27] Mary Smith, an ardent campaigner for poor women's education, wrote a 116-page Spenserian epic entitled 'Progress', possibly influenced by Thomas Cooper's *Purgatory of Suicides*, in which she offered homage to 'all that prospers peace and wakens thought'.

> The men who've blest the ages, made them bright.
> 'Tis men that make earth's history, men who speak
> The everlasting truth that gives earth light.
> Let but a man be born, upright, divine –
> Poet, or saint, or seer – and straight shall shine
> New light on all men; and that one man's power
> Shall thrill the world's heart in its crowning hour.[28]

Blank verse, that ubiquitous nineteenth-century form, was relatively rare in working-class women's verse – a mark, perhaps, of the high regard in which rhyme was held in an oral and musical poetic culture. A rare exception was Agnes Mabon's 'The Drunkard's Inhumanity', an essay in verse whose speaker exclaims:

> Oh! say, can one deserve the name of man
> Who lifts his hand against his bosom's mate? […]
> And listen to his plea, his base defence:
> 'I was in drink', he says, 'she should have known
> To hold her peace, and not arouse me then;
> Nought irritates me like a woman's tongue' […][29]

Other experimenters struck out in other directions. The 'rustic maid' Jane Stevenson (n.d., fl. 1870), who had no formal education, wrote a kind of free verse, which she 'suppose[d]' was 'not prose, and I am not such a judge of poetry as to know whether it may be called poetry or not, or some kind of mixture of both'.

> I may be prejudic'd, this is my birthplace,
> Spot where I have spent my life from earliest infancy;
> Nurs'd up amongst the scenes I have describ'd,
> And seldom mixing with mankind in mutual converse.
> A wild and solitary thing have thus contract
> A love for things inanimate […] ('Home')[30]

Elizabeth Campbell found a natural anapaestic cadence, accompanied by slant rhymes in which she expressed a universal ideal:

> I weep for the coward, I weep for the brave,
> I weep for the monarch, I weep for the slave,
> I weep for all those that in battle are slain,
> I've a tear and a prayer for the souls of all men. ('The Crimean War')[31]

Eliza Cook (1812–89), an accomplished metrist, used seven-beat lines to create a kind of vigorous poetic tracking shot:

> I saw the foreign 'image-man' set down his laden stand;
> I lingered there; and coveted the Beauty that I scanned:
> The 'Dancing Girl', the 'Prancing Steed', the 'Gladiator' dying,
> The bust of 'Milton' close beside where sinless 'Eve' was lying;
> And how I gazed with rapture on the 'Bard of Avon's' face,
> With young, impulsive worship of its majesty and grace. ('The Streets')[32]

For Scottish poets, especially, the poetry of Robert Burns provided models in stanza form as well as content. Jeannie Paterson's 'To One Who Believes that Women are Soulless', for example, addresses 'Willie' in the metres of 'To a Mouse':

> Feith, Willie lad ye gied it braid,
> Richt oot ye spak' it, ay, ye said,
> And this affirmed, that woman, made
>   Was wi' no soul;
> That in the narrow grave when laid
>   That was the goal.[33]

Ethel Carnie (1886–1962), finally, paid homage to Swinburne's ecstatic cadences in the hexameter couplets of 'Immortality':

> The best thoughts we are thinking to-day shall be living and active and strong,
> When we sleep at the end of the fight, caring not for the war-whoop or song,
> And it matters far more than we know that we keep our hearts steadfast and brave,
> For the strength that they held shall walk forth when they mix with the dust of the grave,

And immortal, and lovely, and young shall our dream live unclouded by tears,
When we take the long rest that is sweet after toil in a hundred years.[34]

Drawing on deep oral traditions, all the rural working-class women poets I have studied – as well as many of their urban sisters – composed poetic 'songs'. Ellen Johnston devoted a special section of her volume to such songs, suggesting airs for their accompaniment, and Marion Bernstein (1846–1906), a piano teacher, identified several of her poems as songs or hymns to be 'set to music'.[35] Eliza Cook (1812–89), Ruth Wills, Jeannie Paterson and Ethel Carnie wrote songs with specific suggestions for their accompaniment, and Carnie's 'Marching Tune' was given an original setting by the suffragist composer Ethel Smythe in 1913.

Working-class autobiographers recorded the powerful influence of songs they heard in childhood. Janet Hamilton, for example, once recalled that 'I was beginning to get rich [at age eight] in the Ballad treasures of my country … and a pathetic "Aul Warl Ballant", would put the sweetie shop to a discount at any time when I was mistress of a bawbee'.[36] Traces of English oral and balladic traditions also lingered in the title of poems which were (presumably) not sung, such as Carnie's 'A Riding Song' and Cook's 'Song of the Red Man', and many working-class women poets wrote verse in ballad-stanza form, such as Elizabeth Campbell's 'The Graves of My Sons', Ruth Wills' 'Zenobia', and Ellen Johnston's 'Letter to Edith'.[37] But the period's most strikingly authentic as well as idiosyncratic oral work in ballad form was surely Mary MacPherson's (1821–98) 'Incitement of the Gaels', a chanted Gaelic epic in which rebellious Highland crofters routed government agents sent to evict them from their homes.[38]

> When the landlords gathered round
>   assembled in the county town,
> 'twill be recalled in every age,
>   the tricks they practiced to deceive us […] (ll. 25–32)[39]

A Working-Class Form: 'Ballads of Memorie'

Perhaps the most distinctive subgenre in the poetry of nineteenth-century working-class women was the 'ballad of memorie'. Such 'ballads' took several forms – personal reminiscences, 'people's histories' and 'return ballads', in which an older woman revisited her girlhood home and reflected on the upheavals she and others in her region had endured.

Some of the reminiscence ballads recorded epiphanic experiences, such as Jane Stevenson's encounter with a soothsaying stranger in 'The Prophetess, Or Seer of Visions', whose sense of awe or benediction lingered as a kind of spiritual presence which conferred the poet's authority to speak.

> This is no fiction that I tell,
> Were all her prophecies but half as true
> As is this tale I've told to you,
> Then we had need to be upon our guard,
> If the sad stroke of this calamity
> We possibly may blunt or ward […]
> Ah Scotland! It were well for thee
> If a false prophetess this woman be […]
> But great disasters soon enough may come,
> Without a prophetess foretelling them.[40]

Ballads of 'people's history' also expressed a preference for 'truth' and 'truth-telling' over fiction and a deeply felt need to commemorate those 'forgot by e'en tradition's garrulous tongue', as Mary Smith put it.[41] Aged storytellers had special authority in this genre, and Janet Hamilton was one of its most active practitioners.[42] In 'Grannie's Crack about the Famine in Auld Scotlan' in 1739–40', for example, she expressed a deeply held conviction that striking phenomena or events 'must' have a deeper moral or meaning, if only we are deft enough to interpret them – a poetic variant, perhaps, of the religious typology so cherished by her Dissenting ancestors.

In her 'Crack', a grandfather, angry that his grandchildren have spilled and wasted their food, is mollified when his tactful spouse tells the children a story of elemental faith and stoic desperation in the famine of 1739–40. In that year without harvest, parents had invented games for their children to find bits of vegetables in the dirt, stripped bark off the first shoots of spring trees for food, and watched their friends, neighbours and children die.

> 'An' mony a puir auld man an' wife
> That winter dee't wi' want an' cauld,
> They couldna beg, an' sae their need
> To neebors puir was never tauld.
>
> 'Our Scottish puir had aye some pride –
> An honest, decent pride, I ween;
> Sair want an' sufferin' they thol't
> Ere they wad let their need be seen.

> 'Ae day, I slipp'd my parritch cog [porridge bowl]
> Aneath my jupe, an' ran wi' speed
> To Robin Steel's, for sair I fear'd
> That they had neither meal nor bread.
>
> 'The mither took it in her haun
> An' lifit up to Heaven her e'e,
> An' thankit God for what was gi'en
> Ere she wad let the bairnies pree.
>
> 'That mither – ay, an' mony mair
> That thro' the fiery trials pass'd –
> Like silver seven times purified,
> Cam' oot the furnace pure at last.[43]

Hamilton lived and died within a twenty-mile radius of her home, so it was understandable that long journeys to the other country of the past stirred especially deep emotions when the physical sites she remembered no longer existed.

'Ballads of Return', in which a woman reflected in middle or old age on the upheavals she and others in her region had endured, included Elizabeth Campbell's 'A Summer Night', and 'A Cot By the Moor – A Visit to the Home of my Childhood'; Jane Stevenson's 'Song: The Homes of My Fathers', accompanied by a brief prose account of her foot-journey home and search for her eight brothers and sisters; and Hamilton's 'Feast of the Mutches', in which she attended a public banquet for old women in Glasgow, and reflected on the fates of her childhood friends.

In 'A Wheen Aul' Memories', for example, Hamilton recounted her travels on foot to several once-familiar nearby villages and marked the devastation the smelters had visited on the homes of the literate handloom weavers she remembered from her childhood:

> Noo, mark ye, the ashes, the dross, an' the slag
> Wad ye think it was they put the win' i' the bag
> O' the big millionaires; that 'mang danners an' cinners,
> The Co. should ha'e gather't sic millions o' shiners? (ll. 129–32)[44]

In Mary MacPherson's 'Farewell to the New Christmas', the speaker returned from smoke-choked industrial Glasgow to her beloved native Skye, and was shocked at the island's desolation, 'Where once the honest people lived, only the great sheep and their lambs' (sheep had once again 'devour[ed] men', as More put it three centuries earlier[45]).

> I left the lovely isle of Skye
> more than two score years ago
> and now the custom's altered there
> and sad for me to tell the tale.
>
> Bowed with sadness many a Gael
> bred up in the land of mists
> smothers now in urban streets
> from city dust and reek of coal.

MacPherson's strength deserted her when she came to a stark allegorical sign of this desolation – the ruined family well, painstakingly dug and named by her long-dead father – and she fainted. Fortunately, the well's waters still flowed, and as she drank from them she felt once again her gift's restorative powers ('Tears ebbed away as I began / to sing the melodies I knew'). When members of her community sought to console her with holiday feasting and games, her hopes surged anew:

> When the crowd assembled then,
> that's when a fine din began, […]
> the smiling woman of the house,
> came in to serve a dram around […]
>
> I heard a voice behind me say,
> as one just risen from the grave –
> 'Is not Laclan Og in Ord
> as leader at his people's head.'
>
> We would know again the fields,
> the cornstacks standing in the yard,
> if but the sprit of the folk
> could rise again in hand and heart.[46] (ll. 89–90, 99–100, 105–111)

Personal and communal history fused in this poem, and one imaged the other. The spell in which her 'senses ebbed' offered a bridge from despair to renewal, and its images of redemptive memory new hope that her people's troubles would be mediated, if not healed.

'A Farewell to the New Christmas' abounded, in fact, in concrete, evocative and politically resonant images – a well of healing; flowers of love; an altered state (in which 'her senses ebbed'); a restorative epiphany (which 'brought her spirit to peace'); a strong cup of kindness, and a plangent and redemptive voice from the dead. Merging personal and communal history, it is a crofter's vision of Blake's 'Jerusalem', mediated by William Morris's 'spirit of the folk'.

Were there middle- and upper-class counterparts of such 'ballads of memorie'? Did works such as Morris's *A Dream of John Ball* or Robert Browning's 'The Ring and the Book', steeped in the lore of *The Old Yellow Book* and a sixteenth-century Roman murder trial, restore to our view 'rebel hedge priests' or more urbane Italianate counterparts of lives 'forgotten e'en by tradition's garrulous tongue'?

The answer, in most cases, was 'no'. In works such as Barrett Browning's 'Sonnets from the Portuguese', Rossetti's 'Monna Innominata', or Webster's 'Mother and Daughter', for example, the losses and recoveries evoked were primarily inward, and largely detached from any particular time or place. But there were, I believe, some partial exceptions. William Morris's empathetic historicism and Robert Browning's metaphor of the ring crafted by fire from alloy and gold – resistant unpoetic fact, refashioned by an artist's moral vision – offered 'canonical' (middle-class) responses to the antiphons of personal testimony and collective memory one can hear, from time to time, in the cadences of working-class women's 'ballads of memorie'.

Conclusion

Few working-class women aspired to the complex architectonics of longer 'Parnassian' poems such as *Aurora Leigh*, 'Monna Innominata', or Katherine Bradley and Edith Cooper's long verse dramas, and circumstances of publication and limited audience would have precluded such ambitions in most cases if they had.

Mary Smith, for example, the author of *Progress*, an impressive verse-meditation on the long struggle for social justice, lacked access to sympathetic advice which might have helped her channel her work into less sternly didactic paths. Janet Hamilton also had the self-confidence and ability to create such works. But she was hampered by age – an avid reader and composer of verse in her head, she bore ten children before she learned to write in middle age; and by blindness – she dictated most of her verses and essays after her eyes had failed from a life of work at the loom. Ethel Carnie, finally, an early twentieth-century working-class poet whose nuanced poems convey radical views, later turned to prose fiction in search of a wider popular audience.[47]

What working-class women *did* have was the individual *tessitura* of a collective autobiographical voice; the intensity and autonomy of their lyrical gifts (often carefully nurtured in early childhood); and an ardent desire to add a corrective truth – a dissenting 'memorie' – to more familiar canonical representations of literary consciousness (which they often knew by heart). In their 'ballads of memorie', especially in Hamilton's 'A Wheen Aul' Memories' and MacPherson's 'Farewell to the New Noel' – one can, I believe, hear the haunting alto voice that arrested Gabriel Conroy as the snow fell softly in the dark throughout all Ireland on the gravestones of the dead – not the artfully crafted public sorrow of 'In Memoriam', but a different sort of homage to shared fellowship, solitary courage and the limitless 'fields' we will never know.

Notes

1. In *The Poetry of Chartism: Aesthetics, Politics, History* (Cambridge: Cambridge University Press, 2009), 1, 67, Mike Sanders identifies E.H., 'a factory girl of Stalybridge', and B.T. as women poets who contributed to the *Northern Star* in 1839 and 1838 respectively. For notions of working-class masculinity, see Alexis Easley, 'Ebenezer Elliot and the Construction of Working Class Masculinity', *Victorian Poetry* 39, no. 2 (2001), 303–18 (special issue on 'The Poetics of the Working Classes', ed. Florence Boos).
2. Florence Boos, *Working-Class Women Poets in Victorian Britain: An Anthology* (Peterborough: Broadview, 2008) includes short biographical notices of all the authors discussed here except Agnes Mabon, and a brief bibliography of 40 more working-class women poets who managed to publish their works in hard covers (350–51).
3. Ellen Johnston's 'Rifleman's Melody' (*The Autobiography, Poems and Songs of Ellen Johnston, the 'Factory Girl'* [Glasgow: W. Love, 1867], 40–42) is an exception, but her 'Song of War', set to the tune 'Jeanette and Jeanot', asked 'What is our House of Lords about – our men of Parliament? / They waste their time in passing bills small trifles to prevent; / Let them look at the starving poor – it would be better far / If they would pass a bill for peace, and end this fatal war …' (205–206).
4. The concentration of Scots among working-class women poets whose works have been preserved may have reflected rates of literacy as well as cultural respect for Scottish traditions of 'peoples' poetry'. In *The Rise of Mass Literacy: Reading and Writing in Modern Europe* (Cambridge: Polity, 2000), 10, David Vincent estimated female illiteracy in 1855 at 23 per cent in Scotland and 40 per cent in England. Jeannie Paterson (1871–?)'s *Short Threads from a Milliner's Needle* (Glasgow: Carter & Pratt, 1894) contains a rare dramatic sketch by a working-class woman writer, 'Hereford Castle; or the Rightful Heiress: A Drama'.
5. Consider, for example, Elizabeth Barrett Browning's *Aurora Leigh*, Augusta Webster's 'A Castaway', Christina Rossetti's 'Goblin Market' and 'The Iniquity of the Fathers Upon the Children', May Probyn's 'The Model', and Alice Meynell's 'The Study'.
6. Another exception may be 'One More Bruised Heart!' by the anarchist poet Louisa Sarah Bevington, apparently a protest against child rape.
7. See for example 'Magdalen – A Tale of Christmas Eve', *Ben Brierley's Journal*, December 1871; Boos, *Working-Class Women Poets in Victorian Britain*, 240–41; *Ben Brierley's Journal*, 1 August 1874.
8. Boos, *Working-Class Women Poets in Victorian Britain*, 217–18; Johnston, *Autobiography*, 11.

9. Drawing on records made available by http://scotlandspeople.gov.uk, Gustav Klaus has established that 16-year-old Mary Johnston married Robert Thomson in 1868, and the couple lived with Ellen Johnston at 65 Maitland Street, Glasgow, at the time of the April 1871 census. Klaus, 'New Light on Ellen Johnston, the Factory Girl', *Notes and Queries* no. 55 (2008), 430–33.
10. Johnston, *Autobiography*, 40.
11. The Old Monkland census for 1841 listed Marion Hamilton as a fifteen-year-old girl living with her parents and George Hamilton, her 2-year old son. She appeared in 1861 as Marion Mader, with her son George aged 21, still living with her parents, and in 1881 Marion is listed as Marion Hadyn. Yet the name on George's tombstone is George Hamilton. Since Marion seems to have lived with her parents throughout her life and her son's legal surname was Hamilton, one might surmise that her marital life may have been brief at best.
12. Peter Scheckner, *An Anthology of Chartist Poetry: Poetry of the British Working Class, 1830–1850* (London and Toronto: Associated University Presses, 1989). In W.J. Linton's 'Revenge', a heartless landlord is ambushed and murdered, but though many witness the crime, none betray the doer: 'O Wrong! Thou hast a fearful brood: / What inquest can ye need, / Who know Revenge but reap't the seed / Of blood' (Brian Maidment, *The Poorhouse Fugitives: Self-Taught Poets and Poetry in Victorian Britain* ([Manchester: Carcanet, 1987]), 244). Gerald Massey's 'Song of the Red Republican' exults in the hope of revolutionary vengeance: 'Oh, but 'twill be a merry day, the world shall set apart, / When Strife's last sword is broken in the last crown'd pauper's heart! … Ours is the mighty Future, and what marvel, brother men, / If the devoured of ages should turn devourers, then?' (Maidment, *Poorhouse Fugitives*, 265–66). More subtly, Thomas Cooper's 'Purgatory of Suicides' enjoins, 'Slaves, toil no more! … yea, to the core / Strike their pale craft with paler death!' (Maidment, *Poorhouse Fugitives*, 137).
13. 'The Drunkard's Inhumanity', *Homely Rhymes from the Banks of the Jed* (Paisley, 1887), 145–48.
14. Boos, *Working-Class Women Poets in Victorian Britain*, 71; Janet Hamilton, *Poems, Essays, and Sketches: Comprising the Principal Pieces from her Complete Works* (Glasgow: James Maclehose, 1880), 60.
15. Hamilton, *Poems, Essays and Sketches*, 341.
16. Hamilton, *Poems, Essays and Sketches*, 499–500.
17. Hamilton, *Poems, Essays and Sketches*, 483–84.
18. The 1841 census listed John and Janet Hamilton's oldest son as Archibald Hamilton, age 30, a shoemaker then living at home.
19. See, for example, Frances Power Cobbe, 'Wife-Torture in England', in *Criminals, Idiots, Women and Minors*, ed. Susan Hamilton (Peterborough: Broadview Press, 2004).
20. Boos, *Working-Class Women Poets in Victorian Britain*, 324; Jessie Russell, *The Blinkin' O' The Fire and Other Poems* (Glasgow: Cossar, Fotheringham and Co., 1877), 30. Since the publication of *Working-Class Women Poets* I have learned from Russell's descendants that she and her family emigrated to Marton, New Zealand in 1885, where she became a Salvationist and supporter of women's suffrage.
21. See the discussion in Joan Perkin, *Victorian Women* (New York: New York University Press, 1995), ch. 6, 'Punch and Judy: Holy Deadlock, Separation and Divorce'.
22. For example, Augusta Webster in 'The Castaway' and May Probyn in 'The Model'.
23. Boos, *Working-Class Women Poets in Victorian Britain*, 208; Johnston, *Autobiography*, 100.
24. Other Johnston monologues included 'Lines to the Memory of a Beloved Wife', 'The Lass O' the Glen', 'Lines on the Death of a Child', 'The Absent Husband', 'The Ruined Heiress', 'Marriage Morning', and 'The Drygate Brae'. Johnston and Forrester seem to have been the working-class women poets who worked most frequently in this genre.

25 Johnston, *Autobiography*, 100 and 127; Forrester, in *Ben Brierley's Journal*, April 1873, 181, and November 1872, 121.
26 Boos, *Working-Class Women Poets in Victorian Britain*, 127; Elizabeth Campbell, *Poems*, 3rd series (Arbroath: Kennedy and Buncle, 1865), 28.
27 Milton and Wordsworth's odes also seem to have influenced other elegies, such as Jeannie Paterson's 'In Memoriam: Councillor John Breeze'.
28 Ruth Wills, *Lays of Lowly Life*, 2nd ed. (London: Simpkin, Marshall and Co., 1861), 92–96; Mary Smith, *Progress and Other Poems* (London and Carlisle, 1873), 61, I, V, iii.
29 Agnes Mabon, *Homely Rhymes from the Banks of the River Jed* (Paisley, 1887), 145–46; see also Ethel Carnie's 'A Vision', *Voices of Womanhood* (London: Headley Brothers, n. d. [1911]).
30 Boos, *Working-Class Women Poets in Victorian Britain*, 149; n.a. [Jane Stevenson], *Homely Musings of a Rustic Maiden* (Kilmarnock, 1870), 30.
31 Boos, *Working-Class Women Poets in Victorian Britain*, 128; Elizabeth Campbell, *Poems*, fourth series (Arbroath, 1867), 24.
32 Boos, *Working-Class Women Poets in Victorian Britain*, 284; Eliza Cook, *Poetical Works* (London, 1870), 973. Seven-beat lines were also favoured by Ruth Wills and Jeannie Paterson.
33 Paterson, *Short Threads*, 139.
34 Ethel Carnie, *Songs of a Factory Girl* (London: Headley Brothers, n.d. [1911]), 46–47.
35 Marion Bernstein, *Mirren's Musings, A Collection of Songs and Poems* (Glasgow: MacGeachy, 1876). 'Soaring Upwards to the Light' is glossed as 'Song, set to Music', and 'Move On!' and 'The Music of the Streets' are subtitled 'Song for Music'.
36 Boos, *Working-Class Women Poets in Victorian Britain*, 90; Hamilton, 'Preface', *Poems, Essays and Sketches*. Indirectly, Hamilton's remark also rendered homage to balladic traditions mediated by Robert Fergusson, Allan Ramsay, Walter Scott, Robert Burns and James Hogg.
37 Others, such as 'Mary Lee: A Ballad' (Campbell) and 'The Ballad of the Monkland Cottar' (Hamilton) were specifically crafted as extended third-person narratives.
38 The only scholarly discussion I have found of MacPherson's Gaelic poetry is Donald Eachann Meek's 'Gaelic Poets of the Land Agitation', *Transactions of the Gaelic Society of Inverness*, 49 (1977): 309–76. Meek asserts that 'the peaks and troughs of her own emotions are all too clearly reflected in the uneven texture of her verse', but adds that '[h]er verse therefore contains an emotional drive unmatched in contemporary songs' (314).
39 Boos, *Working-Class Women Poets in Victorian Britain*, 178–81; *The Poetry of Scotland: Gaelic, Scots, and English*, ed. Roderick Watson, trans. William Neill (Edinburgh: Edinburgh University Press, 1995), 495.
40 Boos, *Working-Class Women Poets in Victorian Britain*, 155–56; Jane Stevenson, *Homely Musings*, 109–10. A quasi-'Presbyterian' variant of this chiliastic warning may be found in 'Grannie's Dream', by Hamilton, *Poems, Essays and Sketches*, in which
    A muckle haun, nocht but a haun,
     Was lyin' on the floor outspread;
    A haun as big as ony ten,
     The colour o't a bluidy red [...]
    A soun' mair loud than thunner far,
     Rang through the air aroun', abroad;
    An' whan it ceas'ed, an awfu' voice
     Bade me prepare to meet my God. (ll. 39–44, 49–52)
41 Boos, *Working-Class Women Poets in Victorian Britain*, 311; Smith, *Progress and Other Poems*, 72: I, V, xxxi.

42 Hamilton's commemorations of Scottish Covenanter resistance included 'Bothwell Brig', 'The Ballad of the Monkland Cottar', 'Gran'faither at Cam'slang', 'Some Incidents in the Latter Days of John Whitelaw', 'The Ballad of the New Monkland Martyr' and 'A Real Incident of the Persecuting Times in Scotland', and her homages to her 'Grannie' – the family storyteller – include 'Grannie's Dream: A True Incident', 'Grannie Visited at Blackhill, Shotts, July, 1805', and 'Grannie's Tale: A Ballad O'Memorie'.
43 Hamilton, *Poems, Essays, and Sketches*, 283–84.
44 Boos, *Working-Class Women Poets in Victorian Britain*, 68; Hamilton, *Poems, Essays, and Sketches*, 169.
45 Thomas More, *Utopia* (New York: Norton, 1975), 14: 'Your sheep … used to be so meek and eat so little. Now they are becoming so greedy and wild that they devour men themselves, as I hear.'
46 Boos, *Working-Class Women Poets in Victorian Britain*, 183–84; *The Poetry of Scotland*, 495.
47 For a defence of this view, see Robert Smalley, 'The Life and Work of Ethel Carnie Holdsworth, With Particular Reference to the Period 1907 to 1931', PhD diss., 2 vols, University of Central Lancashire, 2006.

Genre Matters: Attending to Form and Convention in Eighteenth-Century Labouring-Class Poetry
William J. Christmas

To say that genre mattered to eighteenth-century poets, their poems, and their readers is undoubtedly to understate the case. Genre, or poetic kind, often announced in poem titles and defined by recognisable conventions within a poem, was crucial to understanding poetic purpose, influencing readerly response, and, hence, establishing how a given poem means. For a poem titled 'Corydon and Pastora', genre just might be the most salient aspect of its content, whereas 'To Lucinda' would signal a great deal more latitude as to topic within the verse epistle form. Because poetry was an intensely public medium in eighteenth-century Britain, a poem's generic form, or perhaps especially the self-conscious mixing of forms within a single poem, could potentially serve a variety of social, ideological, or political purposes. What makes eighteenth-century poetry so interesting, then as now, has much to do with genre, and perhaps especially the play with genre, form, and poetic convention that so many of the period's poets engaged in.

Recently published work in the field points toward a resurgence of interest in the implications of genre and the heuristics of form and convention for a wider range of poets. David Fairer's revisionist history of eighteenth-century English poetry is noteworthy for its consistent attention to period poetic 'modes' and the uses that a catalogue of poets worthy of a Roger Lonsdale anthology makes of them.[1] The phrase 'inventing genre' ends the subtitle of Paula Backscheider's award-winning study of eighteenth-century women's poetry which focuses, in large measure, on the ways women poets revised existing poetic forms and conventions to carve out their own artistic and personal space.[2] Labouring-class studies has been particularly attuned to this trend: two new books, by Bridget Keegan and Anne Milne, attend to poetic genre in important ways in their analyses of labouring-class nature poetry and representations of domestic animals in labouring-class women's poems respectively.[3] In what follows, I would like to consider what this critical turn toward aesthetics and an historically situated formalism[4] – especially with regard to poetic genre, form, and convention – means for labouring-class studies, and sketch out several avenues for future work.

One of the revelations, for me, in working on the three-volume anthology *Eighteenth-Century English Labouring-Class Poets*, was becoming more acutely aware of just how many *kinds* of poems labouring-class poets produced.[5] Not having to worry about including the Popes and Johnsons of the eighteenth-century poetic world meant that we had the space to focus on representing labouring-class poets' wider engagement with the popular verse forms of the period. This meant paying attention to genre in different ways, which would then potentially allow for new and interesting questions to be asked of labouring-class poetry. If content – traditionally construed as verse of socio-historical or autobiographical value for labouring-class poets – was all that mattered, one might have excerpted Stephen Duck's long 1736 poem, 'A Description of a Journey to Marlborough, Bath, Portsmouth, &c.', pulling out the section where Duck represents himself returning to the Wiltshire countryside for the first time since becoming a patronised court poet. But the 'journey' poem was also a particular kind of topographical verse popular in the first half of the eighteenth century and, to fully understand Duck's achievement, the whole poem must be read in the context of other 'journey' poems produced by a wide range of poets, including other labouring-class ones (e.g. Mary Masters' 'A Journey from Otley to Wakefield' and William Vernon's 'A Journey to Wales').

A critical focus on poetic genre means taking a fresh look at poems still largely ignored, even in our new literary histories, and recalibrating our analytical focus with regard to form and content, or more precisely, form's relationship to content and the ways meaning is constructed. Open up any recent revisionist anthology of eighteenth-century poetry and one is confronted with various kinds of odes, epistles, pastorals, elegies and satires. But what of the vast sea of religious verse popular throughout the period? Perhaps no poetic kind offers up more sub-kinds in the eighteenth century than religious verse, and several of these, like hymns, biblical paraphrastic verse, and psalm translations, were in evidence in countless single-author volumes as well as miscellanies and collections devoted exclusively to these poetic forms. For example, two important anthologies of psalm translations, Henry Dell's *A Select Collection of the Psalms of David* (1756) and Benjamin Williams's *The Book of Psalms, as Translated, Paraphrased, or Imitated by Some of the Most Eminent English Poets* (1781), include ample selections from both women (Elizabeths Rowe, Tollet, and Carter) and labouring-class poets (Masters, Thomas Blacklock, and Mary Leapor), and these names are featured prominently on their respective title pages along with John Milton, Joseph Addison, and Isaac Watts. It is eminently clear that eighteenth-century readers valued this verse far more than we do (and made less of a fuss about including women and labouring-class contributors in this context), though modern critics are starting to incorporate significant analysis of religious verse into their new literary histories.[6]

Masters' poem, 'The 37th Psalm. Inscrib'd to an Injur'd Friend', offers a useful test case for understanding the complex, often subtle relationship between form, content, and meaning in what tends to be a highly conventional period poetic mode in the eighteenth century: psalm translation. Masters wrote a great deal of biblical paraphrastic verse and generally favoured religious themes in her poetry. Discouraged from the classical tradition by her father, Masters turned to the Bible for poetic inspiration and raw material. It helped, of course, that devotional verse of all kinds was widely appreciated, practised, and consumed throughout the eighteenth century. Several influential male critics and poets in the early-century period – Addison, John Dennis, and Richard Blackmore among them – defined 'true Poetry' as that concerned with Christian themes and salvation, and called for more poets to write in this vein. In writing so much pious verse, Masters was no doubt being true to herself, but it was also a shrewd move as the field of 'divine poetry' offered a far greater degree of freedom and independence for a woman with literary aspirations. And, as Patricia Phillips has noted, religious poetry by women more often 'escaped the censure of serious men'.[7] One of Masters' supporters, Thomas Scott, says as much in celebrating her psalm translations:

> And let your fair Translations show
> What Beauties in the Scriptures grow: [...]
> Then Wits in silence shall admire
> Isaiah's more than Homer's Fire;
>   Pindar to David yield the Prize,
> And Virgil's Majesty in Moses rise.[8]

Scott suggests that by eschewing classical authors for biblical heroes in her poetry, Masters can in effect silence those 'Wits' predisposed to criticise female education and women's writing on subjects beyond the Bible. Manipulating the forms and conventions of eighteenth-century religious verse, women poets like Masters could both largely keep within the confines of masculine conceptions of femininity in the period, and (potentially) still represent female experience on the public stage.

Masters' translation of psalm 37 appeared first in her 1733 volume, *Poems on Several Occasions*. The poem was later collected in George Colman and Bonnell Thornton's anthology, *Poems by Eminent Ladies* (1755), and subsequently picked up by both Dell and Williams in their collections of psalm translations mentioned above. Psalm 37 is categorised as a wisdom-type psalm that centres on the theme of retribution; the notion that all evildoers, no matter how prosperous, shall meet an untimely demise, and that the righteous, no matter how poor, shall inherit the earth is repeated several times. Given the repetition of language and imagery to do with material wealth, poverty, agriculture, and property, the psalmist clearly had what we might call a 'class' context in mind. But in her translation of this psalm, I want to suggest that Masters accommodates the biblical text to another contemporary social context of iniquity: gender. In his recent book on seventeenth-century psalters, Hannibal Hamlin points out that early-modern poets engaged in a process of 'free paraphrase', often adapting the biblical text to their own situations and concerns.[9] To understand this process as a kind of translation, as Hamlin does, is to raise specific questions worth pursuing as critics: How does the poet 'read' the biblical text? What interpretive openings are exploited in the translation? What aesthetic, theological, ideological, and/or historical latitudes are taken by the poet-as-translator?

If, as the cliché goes, every translation involves interpretation, then close comparative analysis is key to revealing how Masters is reading a given psalm and potentially refiguring it in her own verse translation. There are several cues in Masters' version of psalm 37 that allow for a distinctly gender-focused interpretation of her intentions. First, Masters takes the standard biblical subtitle, 'A Psalm of David', and replaces it with 'Inscrib'd to an Injured Friend'.[10] One obvious effect of this revision is to place her psalm translation into the context of the eighteenth-century verse epistle, the form Masters (and many others) used almost exclusively when addressing poems to pseudonymous female friends.[11] Given that Masters' 1733 volume contains many such poems, one is inclined, from the altered subtitle alone, to read Masters' translation of psalm 37 as a kind of 'female friendship' poem. Here the subtitle becomes a prominent marker of generic hybridisation that signals to the reader a greater latitude with regard to topical content and, hence, potential meaning beyond the merely religious or devotional.

This particular psalm, in which David addresses the reader and speaks in the first person, lends itself well to the verse epistle form. But Masters is stretching the biblical text in terms of both gender and voice. It seems that Masters' speaker is not David, but a woman writing to a female friend who has been 'injur'd', or wronged, in some way, probably by a man. The psalm opens 'Fret not thyself because of evildoers, neither be thou envious against the workers of iniquity' (Psalms 37:1). Masters rewrites this opening as follows: 'Fret not thyself when wicked Men prevail,/And bold Iniquity bears down the Scale'.[12] In the first line, Masters sticks close to the source text, maintaining the gender-neutral 'thyself', but then veers from it markedly by specifying the biblical psalmist's generic 'evildoers' as 'wicked Men'. And in her second line, Masters jettisons the idea that the righteous might be jealous of the prosperity of the wicked in favour of a broader sociological point that practically personifies 'Iniquity' as a force which 'bears down the Scale', effectively tipping the balance of gender power toward men.

To follow this line of thinking through Masters' translation is to understand the poet reading the biblical text as a woman, exploiting its interpretive possibilities, and rewriting this psalm of retribution as advice to a fellow woman, offering it as a kind of palliative to a wronged female friend. Though the righteous are generically represented as 'men' in Masters' poem, they are associated with the contemporary discourse of 'virtue', with all of its attendant feminised associations, while the wicked are consistently figured in masculinised metaphors like 'potent villains' and 'sons of vice'.[13] In this context, the climactic and often quoted verse of the biblical text – 'For such as be blessed of him shall inherit the earth; and they that be cursed of him shall be cut off' (Psalms 37:22) – becomes a kind of fantasy of female power for Masters:

> And Pow'r, unknown before, shall bless thy Hand.
> Thy late insulting Foe to thee shall bend,
> And thou shalt mark his miserable End.[14]

Masters' imagery is certainly more explicit than that of the source text, allowing the reader to picture her 'injur'd Friend' considering the forms that 'bend[ing]' and 'miserable End' might take. What Masters seems to want to say in this poem about gender, power, and the plight of women under patriarchy might have been readily fitted into a hard-hitting verse epistle, so opting for a popular religious form, and the generic hybridity her full title suggests, seems a particularly self-conscious artistic choice. This poem's extended social life beyond its original publication, in the specialised collections noted above, illustrates the ways that even a labouring-class woman could manipulate readerly expectations of poetic form and convention to speak as a woman to women, and still gain a wider audience.

I hope that this reading of Masters' translation of psalm 37 is suggestive of a kind of work still needing to be done in the field of labouring-class poetry. Until very recently, the corpus of labouring-class poetry produced in the eighteenth century has been mined, almost exclusively, for those poems that represent historical aspects of labouring-class experience and identity. Returning to the same volumes of verse that provided 'The Thresher's Labour' or 'Crumble-Hall' and rereading with an *interest* in generic form and convention, could yield important results. One might notice, for example, how many labouring-class poets throughout the century wrote animal verse fables. John Bancks, Mary Masters, Robert Dodsley, Stephen Duck, and Mary Leapor all worked in this form which was both popular and had literary cachet in the period, thanks to translations of Æsop by Sir Roger L'Estrange and John Dryden, critical commentary by Dennis, Blackmore and Addison aligning the fable with both 'wit' and the Homeric epic, and well-known efforts by Scriblerians like John Gay.[15] Mark Loveridge notes that there is a rich tradition of 'eclectic and subversive' fables published in the first decades of the eighteenth century that gives way, after Gay's *Fables* (1727), to an expanding conservative tradition upholding dominant or normative values.[16] How do verse fables by labouring-class poets fit into, or complicate, this literary history? If the animal verse fable was another of those neoclassical 'master texts', like the pastoral or irregular ode, that served as training ground for fledgling poets, how did labouring-class poets use or transform this form (as they often did others) to serve their own purposes? The many labouring-class examples of this popular poetic kind have so far escaped modern critical notice, though, as is the case with labouring-class psalm translations, certain of these poems, like Duck's 'The Two Beavers', did enjoy periodical publication and anthological afterlife in the eighteenth century.[17]

When genre does figure in our analyses of labouring-class poetry, there is an observable tendency to focus on generic 'exceptionalism' or, more specifically given eighteenth-century poetic practices, generic innovation and hybridity. The chapters of Bridget Keegan's fine study, *British Labouring-Class Nature Poetry, 1730–1837*, are organised around particular 'subgenres' of nature poetry, like the garden poem and the prospect poem. Though Keegan remains sensitive to the many moments in such poems that do not measure up, her central argument is grounded in ferreting out generic innovation: 'From Stephen Duck's *The Thresher's Labour* (1730) to John Clare's enclosure elegies of the 1830s, labouring-class poetry makes significant innovations in the modes available for writing poetry about nature.'[18] Although she employs a different methodological strategy, Anne Milne is nevertheless also interested in generic form and innovation. Her chapter on Elizabeth Hands, for example, is centred on Hands' short poem, 'Written, originally extempore, on seeing a Mad Heifer run through the Village where the Author Lives', and argues for the ways Hands puts both form (the 'extempore' mode) and content (the heifer) 'to subversive use'.[19] Hands' poem turns out to be doubly exceptional: not only singled out by Milne from a tradition of extempore poems, even those by other women labouring-class poets like Masters, but also defined by the author *vis-à-vis* her title, 'Written, originally extempore', as simultaneously of, and not of, that poetic kind. My own reading of Masters' translation of psalm 37 above is also linked in obvious ways to this not-yet-exhausted critical trend of examining exceptional or innovative labouring-class poems within specific generic and thematic contexts.

But what of generic 'sameness' and uber-conventionality? Speaking of Duck to their mutual friend, Joseph Spence, Alexander Pope opined that the thresher-poet's early work showed 'no imagination, all imitation'.[20] This might not be the utterly disparaging comment it is usually taken to be; it might simply be accurate. Apart from 'The Thresher's Labour', which offers evidence of authorial play with a variety of poetic forms and conventions, the vast majority of Duck's poems fit into clearly defined generic moulds. We might then ask critical questions that would not necessarily be the ones Pope and his contemporaries would have asked, but that I think we should ask in our attempts to come to a fuller understanding both of eighteenth-century poetics and of individual poets like Duck: Are conventional poems by labouring-class authors merely exercises in conventionality? What 'work' do such poems do, both with regard to eighteenth-century society at large, and for the poets themselves? What might we say about such conventional poems (traditionally considered uninteresting, insipid, or worse) through an historically attuned formalist methodology? To read many labouring-class pastorals, epigrams, verse panegyrics, or imitations of classical authors as more than perfunctory exercises in prosody will require jettisoning – or at least seriously rethinking – definitions of poetic value inherited from Pope and the Romantics. That, I suggest, will be no easy task, for the poems that would count as 'conventional' in this scenario could not be 'exceptional' or 'innovative', terms which, in spite of their canon-cracking use-value, nevertheless still carry the conceptual weight of poetic imagination and originality. But I see much of the recent work in the field of eighteenth-century poetics, with its focus on genre and employing what I am calling an 'historically situated formalism', furthering the recovery process by widening our view of eighteenth-century poems worth reading and talking about. My sense is that a vast array of conventional, and seemingly conventional, poems are still out there in the archives awaiting the attention of this, and subsequent, generations of scholars.

Notes

1   David Fairer, *English Poetry of the Eighteenth Century 1700–1789* (London: Longman, 2003), x.
2   Paula R. Backscheider, *Eighteenth-Century Women Poets and Their Poetry: Inventing Agency, Inventing Genre* (Baltimore, MD: Johns Hopkins University Press, 2005).
3   See Bridget Keegan, *British Labouring-Class Nature Poetry, 1730–1837* (Houndmills and New York: Palgrave Macmillan, 2008), and Anne Milne, *'Lactilla Tends her Fav'rite Cow': Ecocritical Readings of Animals and Women in Eighteenth-Century British Labouring-Class Women's Poetry* (Lewisburg, PA: Bucknell University Press, 2008).
4   My use of this phrase is informed by Susan Wolfson's pioneering work, *Formal Charges: The Shaping of Poetry in British Romanticism* (Stanford: Stanford University Press, 1997), esp. 1–30, and by J. Paul Hunter's work on the couplet. See his 'Formalism and History: Binarism and the Anglophone Couplet', *Modern Language Quarterly* 61 no. 1 (March 2000; special issue on 'Formalism', ed. Marshall Brown and Susan Wolfson), 109–29 and 'Sleeping Beauties: Are Historical Aesthetics Worth Recovering?', *Eighteenth-Century Studies* 34 no. 1 (Fall 2000), 1–20.

5   See *Eighteenth-Century English Labouring-Class Poets, 1700–1800*, ed. William Christmas, Bridget Keegan and Tim Burke (London: Pickering & Chatto, 2003), gen. ed. John Goodridge, 3 volumes.
6   See, for example, Backscheider's chapter 'Hymns, Narratives, and Innovations in Religious Poetry' in *Eighteenth-Century Women Poets*, 123–74; Bridget Keegan, 'Mysticisms and Mystifications: The Demands of Labouring-Class Religious Poetry', *Criticism* 47 no. 4 (2005), 471–91; and Emma Mason, 'Poetry and Religion', in *A Companion to Eighteenth-Century Poetry*, ed. Christine Gerrard (Oxford: Blackwell, 2006), 53–68.
7   Patricia Phillips, *The Adventurous Muse: Theories of Originality in English Poetics, 1650–1760* (Uppsala & Stockholm: Almqvist & Wiksell International, 1984), 8.
8   T[homas] S[cott], 'To Mrs. Masters, upon reading the 139th Psalm turned into Verse by her', in Mary Masters, *Poems on Several Occasions* (London, 1733), 235.
9   Hannibal Hamlin, *Psalm Culture and Early Modern English Literature* (Cambridge: Cambridge University Press, 2004), 11–12.
10 Masters, *Poems on Several Occasions*, 177.
11 For an excellent account of the verse epistle in this period, see Bill Overton, *The Eighteenth-Century British Verse Epistle* (Houndmills and New York: Palgrave Macmillan, 2007). Overton notes of Masters that 'although her two collections embrace only a few poems entitled 'Epistle', they also contain [...] much social/moral verse that has an epistolary character' (60–1). Certainly this psalm translation has an 'epistolary character' too.
12 Masters, *Poems on Several Occasions*, 177.
13 Masters, *Poems on Several Occasions*, 184; 178.
14 Masters, *Poems on Several Occasions*, 184.
15 Mark Loveridge, *A History of Augustan Fable* (Cambridge: Cambridge University Press, 1998), 41–2.
16 Loveridge, *History of Augustan Fable*, 40–1.
17 'The Two Beavers' appeared in the first number of *The Museum; or, The Literary and Historical Register* (March 1746), 295–97, a periodical founded by Robert Dodsley and edited by Mark Akenside. The poem was subsequently published in the third edition of Duck's *Poems on Several Occasions* (London, 1753; reissued 1764). The poem then appeared in Dodsley's *A Collection of Poems in Six Volumes*, from the 1765 edition onwards.
18 Keegan, *British Labouring-Class Nature Poetry*, 37.
19 Milne, 'Lactilla Tends her Fav'rite Cow', 69.
20 Joseph Spence, *Observations, Anecdotes, and Characters of Books and Men, Collected from Conversation*, vol. I, ed. James M. Osborn (Oxford: Clarendon Press, 1966), 215.

Ecocriticism
Anne Milne

There is an abundance of landscape, elemental nature imagery, and representations of the natural world in the poetry of eighteenth-century labouring-class poets. The reality is that many of these poets lived largely outdoors engaged in various forms of agricultural labour. Though the intricacies of farm labour as labour and the aesthetic traditions and political conditions from which landscapes in labouring-class poetry arose have been skilfully teased out by critics such as John Goodridge and John Barrell, I feel that the specific natures, in which and out of which these poets lived and worked and wrote, still need to be probed through a literary critical perspective that can potentially offer new insights.[1] This impulse to be attentive to nature in literary texts is in keeping with Raymond Williams's assertion that nature is 'perhaps the most complex word in the language'.[2] Indeed, if we adhere to Williams's first sense of the word 'nature', it is useful to consider whether the 'nature' of labouring-class poetry, its 'essential quality' in Williams's words, lies in its relation 'to the material world itself'.[3] This shift to an ecocentric perspective foregrounds the relationships between the literary and the natural worlds. This enacts a radical reassessment by transforming what is traditionally read in literary studies as 'setting' to an ecocritical rereading as 'place'.

A more pointed attentiveness to 'place' in literary studies reveals relationships to the land and other living creatures, emotional ties to nature, marks of history and change on the land, and, perhaps, most importantly, the rootedness of poetry in *specific* places. This bioregional orientation not only enables the literary critic to identify and pinpoint place based on geographical and biological markers such as weather and specific indigenous plants and animals, it underlines a sense of belonging-in-place that belies common class-based exclusionary practices enacted upon labouring-class poets and, indeed, deeply legitimises and authorises them to speak of, in, and about place and their specific and special relationship to it. As Madeline Kahn has pointed out in her comparison of Wordsworth and Ann Yearsley, 'Yearsley is not standing in the same place as Wordsworth'.[4] Though Kahn may be in part employing metaphor when she refers to 'place' here, ecocriticism emphasises the importance of pausing to see that place fully *as* place. In this way, *where* Stephen Duck threshes and *where* Ann Yearsley as 'LACTILLA half sunk in snow … tends her fav'rite cow' matters both generally and in its bioregional specificity.[5]

If, then, the way in which labouring-class poets inhabit place differs from those of other poets, an ecocritical approach can also help to illuminate their texts in several other respects. For example, Peter Barry has suggested that attentiveness to land use in literary texts blurs the nature/culture binary and challenges the impulse to assert that nature is socially constructed, reducible and '"always already" textualised into "discourse"'.[6] This invites a consideration of the 'toxic consciousness' present in literary texts both in the way that texts internalise and normalise disruptive land uses and in the way that land use policies and priorities in the eighteenth century literally lay the groundwork for future land use practices and conceptualisations of nature. Here, ecocriticism becomes a useful partner with other critical practices such as Marxism, feminism, and cultural studies in probing what are sometimes called 'interlocking oppressions'. Under this rubric, then, Lactilla's cow and the weather in Duck's expression of the thresher's working day, for example, become important agents of enquiry focusing and forcing the critic to consider not only how animals and weather are represented and what they represent but when and why they are represented in these specific ways. It is easy to see that by merely introducing these potential correspondences, ecocriticism aids in both illuminating the complexity of labouring-class texts and in enabling the multiple depths and layers present in these poems to be read. Ultimately, ecocritical attention to land use and ecocentric environmental principles such as 'growth and energy, balance and imbalance, symbiosis and mutuality, and sustainable or unsustainable uses of energy and resources'[7] returns the study of the work of labouring-class poets in the eighteenth century to its roots in order to reinforce and underline the discourses of class within eighteenth-century poetry, but with a richer context in the inescapable groundedness of our human experiences as natural beings in the natural world.

Notes

1 John Goodridge, *Rural Life in Eighteenth-Century English Poetry.* (Cambridge: Cambridge University Press, 1995); John Barrell, *The Dark Side of the Landscape: The Rural Poor in English Painting, 1730–1840* (Cambridge: Cambridge University Press, 1980).
2 Raymond Williams, *Keywords: A Vocabulary of Culture and Society* (Oxford: Oxford University Press, 1983), 219.
3 Williams, *Keywords*, 219.
4 Madeline Kahn, 'The Milkmaid's Voice: Ann Yearsley and the Romantic Notion of the Poet', in *Approaches to Teaching British Women Poets of the Romantic Period*, ed. Stephen C. Behrendt and Harriet Kramer Linkin (New York: MLA, 1997), 144.
5 Stephen Duck, 'The Thresher's Labour' in *The Thresher's Labour and The Woman's Labour* (1730; Los Angeles: University of California Press, 1985); Ann Yearsley, 'Clifton Hill', *Poems on Several Occasions* (London: G.G.J. & J. Robinson, 1785).
6 Peter Barry, *Beginning Theory: An Introduction to Literary and Cultural Theory* (Manchester: Manchester University Press, 2009, 3rd edn), 243.
7 Peter Barry, *Beginning Theory*, 254.

The Rise of Robert Bloomfield
Scott McEathron

Upon reading Robert Bloomfield's newly published poem *The Farmer's Boy* in 1800, the essayist Nathan Drake predicted that it 'would confer durable Fame on the first and most polish'd Poet in the Kingdom'. This assessment initially appeared astute: Bloomfield's poem on the Suffolk countryside of his youth went on to sell 26,000 copies in a three-year period and by 1815 was in its thirteenth edition. But gradually Bloomfield's popularity declined, and in the latter decades of the nineteenth century he fell, precipitously, from the canon. Now, two hundred years later, he is back, riding a surge of scholarly interest that is truly remarkable in its scope. Among the developments of this last few years: the first modern critical monograph, Simon White's *Robert Bloomfield, Romanticism and the Poetry of Community*; a major collection of essays, *Robert Bloomfield: Lyric, Class and the Romantic Canon*; a revised and enlarged edition of *Robert Bloomfield: Selected Poems*;[1] a series of articles in top scholarly journals (including pieces by Simon White, Tim Fulford, Debbie Lee, and Theresa Adams); multiple panels at recent meetings of the British Association of Romantic Studies; and the formation of a Robert Bloomfield Society.

Some of the forces helping to stimulate this revival are easy to identify. Most broadly, Bloomfield is benefiting from the general impulse towards recovery and canon-expansion which has swept through Romantic studies, bringing revitalised attention to figures like Mary Robinson, Thomas Moore, and Charlotte Smith, who, like Bloomfield, were popular and important poets in their day. More particularly, Bloomfield is helped by growing interest in labouring-class poetry, a field of study which in recent years has seen an important series of monographs (Landry, Janowitz, Keegan, Christmas, Goodridge);[2] anthologies (*English Labouring-Class Poets*, ed. John Goodridge et al; *Poorhouse Fugitives*, ed. Brian Maidment; *Working-Class Women Poets in Victorian England*, ed. Boos);[3] and major editions *(The Works of Mary Leapor, The Collected Works of James Hogg, The Poems of John Clare*).[4] The Clare connection has been especially important for Bloomfield studies, as Clare's many exponents have been eager to establish commonalities between these two poets of rural England. With Bloomfield thus situated at the meeting-point of several overlapping scholarly impulses, the blossoming interest in his work seems sensible enough.

But if this late rising of Bloomfield is coherent within disciplinary terms, a more complicated follow-up question is whether this attention can reasonably be sustained. A pointed, shadow-version of this query would be: is Bloomfield's substantial corpus – beyond *The Farmer's Boy* – actually rich enough to keep scholars interested? The question is a fair one, but let me suggest that, at least in the short term, the likely test ground for Bloomfield's staying power is not going to be located exclusively, or even primarily, in his poetic corpus.

Instead, the treasure trove – and it is nothing less – is the newly released electronic edition of *The Letters of Robert Bloomfield and His Circle*, edited by Tim Fulford and Lynda Pratt.[5] Fulford and Pratt present a thoroughly annotated edition of 'all his extant letters', supplemented with correspondence from his family and various literary contacts along with contemporary reviews, illustrations, and associated poetic texts. Totalling over 400 letters, the database is searchable (look for the Search button in the upper right hand corner of the frame) and includes an index of correspondents. Fulford and Pratt suggest that, in conjunction with recent scholarly studies, the letters will help make the 'study of Bloomfield properly possible for the first time. […] The hope is that by presenting a properly edited and annotated Collected Letters, we, the editors, will not only foster the infant that is Bloomfield Studies, but also enable him to be a significant figure for all those studying early nineteenth-century literature and culture.'

They suggest several particular avenues of enquiry. Noting Bloomfield's astounding initial popularity and later fall into grave financial distress, Fulford and Pratt see his years of correspondence with publishers, booksellers, and editors as 'vital reading for any critic interested in the book trade and its effect not just on authors but on authors' very conception and practice of authorship'. Relatedly, they describe his frustrating professional position, caught in a swirl of patrons and would-be patrons ranging from Capel Lofft to the Duke of Grafton to, in the 1820s, 'local gentleman [who were trying] to make him conform in print and in private to a loyalist, evangelical and Tory agenda'. These conflicts 'result [in] a long series of letters that exemplify the difficulties of patronage in a manner that all students of Clare, Blake, Wordsworth and Johnson will wish to examine'. Bloomfield also 'received many letters from labouring-class writers, or from middle-class radicals seeking to recruit him as an ally', even as it was frequently true that 'Bloomfield resented those whom he thought had designs upon him'.

Fulford and Pratt also point to Bloomfield's comments on Britain's extended military engagement with France, including early letters that 'captur[e] the animosity that many London artisans felt towards Pitt's bellicose policies which cost the lives of the labouring classes', and later ones that record 'the euphoria of the moment' after the initial defeat of Napoleon in 1814. Having recently published an essay on Bloomfield's poem describing the launch of the warship *Boyne* in 1790 and his subsequent feelings about the war, I can attest that my own work would have benefited enormously from access to this edition.[6]

Aiding Fulford, Pratt, and Goodridge were the technical team of Laura Mandell and Averill Buchanan; Sam Ward, Assistant Editor with a focus on the labouring-class poets; and Carol Bolton, who transcribed many letters. They are to be congratulated on this dazzling resource, freely available to all.

Notes

1. Simon White, *Robert Bloomfield, Romanticism and the Poetry of Community* (Aldershot: Ashgate, 2007); *Robert Bloomfield: Lyric, Class and the Romantic Canon*, ed. Simon White, John Goodridge, and Bridget Keegan (Lewisburg, PA: Bucknell University Press, 2006); *Robert Bloomfield: Selected Poems*, ed. John Goodridge and John Lucas (Nottingham: Trent Editions, 2007).
2. Donna Landry, *The Muses of Resistance: Laboring-Class Women's Poetry in Britain, 1739–1796* (Cambridge: Cambridge University Press, 1990); Anne Janowitz, *Lyric and Labour in the Romantic Tradition* (Cambridge: Cambridge University Press, 1998); Bridget Keegan, *British Labouring-Class Nature Writing, 1730–1837* (Basingstoke: Palgrave Macmillan, 2008); William J. Christmas, *The Lab'ring Muses: Work, Writing, and the Social Order in English Plebeian Poetry, 1730-1830* (Newark and London: University of Delaware Press and Associated University Presses, 2001); Christmas; John Goodridge, *Rural Life in Eighteenth-Century English Poetry* (Cambridge: Cambridge University Press, 1995).
3. *Eighteenth-Century English Labouring-Class Poets, 1700–1800*, ed. William Christmas, Bridget Keegan and Tim Burke (London: Pickering & Chatto, 2003), gen. ed. John Goodridge, 3 volumes; *Nineteenth-Century English Labouring-Class Poets, 1800–1900*, ed. Scott McEathron, Kaye Kossick and John Goodridge (London: Pickering & Chatto, 2006), gen. ed John Goodridge, 3 volumes; *Poorhouse Fugitives*, ed. Brian Maidment (Manchester: Carcanet Press, 1987); *Working-Class Women Poets in Victorian England*, ed. Florence Boos (Peterborough: Broadview, 2008).
4. *The Works of Mary Leapor*, ed. Richard Greene and Ann Messenger (Oxford: Oxford University Press, 2003); *The Collected Works of James Hogg*, gen. eds Douglas S. Mack, Gillian Hughes, Ian Duncan, and Suzanne Gilbert (Edinburgh: Edinburgh University Press, 1995–) 27 vols; *Poems of John Clare*, eds Eric Robinson, David Powell et al. (Oxford: Oxford University Press, 1984–2003), 9 vols.
5. *The Letters of Robert Bloomfield and His Circle*, ed. Tim Fulford and Lynda Pratt, associate editor John Goodridge, available as of September 2009 through the Romantic Circles website, http://www.rc.umd.edu/editions/bloomfield_letters/ (accessed 6 July 2010).
6. Scott McEathron, 'An Infant Poem of War: Bloomfield's "On Seeing the Launch of the Boyne"' in White, Goodridge and Keegan (eds), *Robert Bloomfield*.

The Foresters: Alexander Wilson's Transatlantic Labouring-Class Nature Poetry
Bridget Keegan

The ideological function of eighteenth-century and Romantic British loco-descriptive poetry is axiomatic. From Denham and Pope to Thomson and Jago to Cowper and Wordsworth, in its various incarnations as prospect poetry, georgic poetry, or the poetry of picturesque travel, such verse imagines spaces where the poet might map out an artistic identity and explore questions of history, of national boundaries, and of empire.[1] This essay examines what becomes of the English tradition of writing about landscape when it is uprooted and transplanted transatlantically. The mutual influence that late eighteenth- and early nineteenth-century writers on either side of the Atlantic had on one another has recently been examined by critics such as Susan Manning, Paul Giles, Lance Newman and Joel Pace.[2] While these critics have usefully expanded scholarly boundaries by questioning the limitations of national boundaries for literary enquiry, to date none has investigated the impact of an author's socioeconomic class in transatlantic literary transpositions. The present analysis hopes to address that gap through a reading of Alexander Wilson's loco-descriptive poem, *The Foresters* (first published in serial form in 1809–10). The poem details his journey, taken in the fall of 1804, from outside Philadelphia, Pennsylvania to Niagara Falls, New York. Along his route Wilson encounters productive farmlands, dense forests, sublime mountain vistas, and river and lakeside scenery. The landscape is peopled with settlers of several different European nationalities, farmers, hunters and trappers, and beleaguered schoolmasters. Significantly, Wilson also describes the traces left by the recently dispossessed Native Americans.

The poem is more than mere travelogue. It is a fascinating poetic hybrid, bringing together a variety of discourses, from the scientific to the satirical, and interrogating the transatlantic possibilities of old world forms for new world landscapes. Wilson creates a picturesque and picaresque narrative, incorporating stylistic techniques from Renaissance chorography, prospect and riparian poetry, and the georgic, among others, and figuratively translating these traditionally 'British' forms onto an American geography. The poem incorporates allusions to American and British writers, with Freneau and Franklin on equal footing with Milton and Goldsmith. Just as uniquely, the text is composed by a former weaver and pedlar turned poet, a man from Paisley who redefined himself, as so many immigrants did, upon his arrival in America.

The Foresters and much of Wilson's later poetry written in America are thus useful sources for examining the dissemination and transformation of labouring-class culture in the Atlantic World. Wilson's ambitious long poem allows us to investigate the 'cross-pollination' of discursive and descriptive modes within England, Scotland, and North America. Moreover, the political, social, and natural environments he depicts through his journey force questions of whether the already vexed category of labouring-class poetry can survive the Atlantic crossing. As we consider new directions in the recovery of labouring-class culture and writing, we must begin to account for it more fully and regularly within a *transatlantic* framework, as this was an important context in which such culture was both produced and consumed. As Paul Giles has argued:

> To restore an American dimension to British literature of this period is to denaturalise it, to suggest the historical contingencies that helped formulate the dynamics of Augustan order and imperial control. Conversely, to restore a British dimension to American literature is to politicise it: to reveal its intertwinement with the discourses of heresy, blasphemy, and insurrection, rather than understanding that writing primarily as an expression of local cultures or natural rights.[3]

In the spirit of Giles's observations, I would like to discuss how Wilson's work confirms and complicates our understanding of labouring-class writing in the early nineteenth century. Wilson would go on to make his fame as 'the first American ornithologist', writing numerous poems about birds and producing the epic nine-volume *American Ornithology* that influenced John James Audubon. While he enthusiastically assumes an American identity, Wilson shares many interests with a poet such as Robert Burns (with whom he corresponded) or John Clare. Throughout his poetic career, whether in the work he composed in Scotland or in America, he writes of rural folk culture with a keen ear for the cadences of dialect, and he demonstrates a love for humble life, whether plant, animal, or human.

In addition, as a labouring-class Scottish immigrant who assimilated quickly and enthusiastically to the opportunities afforded by early nineteenth-century America, becoming a citizen in 1804 and embracing a Franklinesque faith in self-improvement and progress, Wilson can be said to stand in the position of both colonised and coloniser. His work allows us to continue considering the appropriateness of postcolonial theories in the reinterpretation of eighteenth- and nineteenth-century labouring-class poetry, and Scottish labouring-class poetry in particular. In her groundbreaking study, *The Muses of Resistance*, Donna Landry was among the first to apply questions of postcolonial critique to labouring-class women writers, in particular Scottish poet Janet Little.[4]

More recently, Gary Harrison has productively applied concepts drawn from postcolonial theory toward understanding John Clare's later poetry.[5] While it may be protested that Scotland was not technically a 'colony' in the same way that, prior to 1776, America was, and that it is thus erroneous to imagine that Wilson saw himself in the position of 'colonised', the subject matter and style of his earliest writing announce their resistance to English cultural imperialism and to the exploitation and marginalisation of labourers' voices within the British Isles. Prior to his immigration Wilson was briefly imprisoned for writing poetry that protested against unfair labour conditions. As Laura Rigal asserts, 'Between 1790 and 1795, Wilson had participated in and struggled directly against British industrial expansion in Scotland'. His poems 'The Hollander or Light-Weight' (1791) and 'The Shark, or Lang Mills Detected' (1793) demonstrate his commitment to radical politics. The latter poem, written in dialect, directly incites workers to rebellion. Rigal comments:

> In the midst of the growing British reaction to the revolution in France and to growing anti-British sentiment in Scotland, Wilson had combined chronic poverty with weaving, book and cloth peddling, the writing of dialect poetry, and radical politics – specifically involvement in a Paineite Jacobin organization called 'The Friends of Liberty and Reform.' Jacobin organizations in industrial west Scotland were able to connect the ideals and events of the French Revolution with Scots artisan/worker resistance to British industrial development, combining artisan-based Scots nationalism with hostility to British commercial and manufacturing expansion.[6]

To escape the possibility of further imprisonment for his supposedly seditious writing, Wilson left Scotland for America in 1794.

While Wilson's Scottish poetry suggests that he might be read as contributing to a broader critique of European internal colonialism, at critical points *The Foresters* appears complicit in an internal colonising process in America, as Wilson follows those who had pushed the American frontier westward, violently pushing out the Native American populations. In describing his travels, on foot or sometimes by boat along the Susquehanna and on the Great Lakes, Wilson's narrator consumes the landscape in the manner of a middle-class picturesque tourist and not a formerly poverty-stricken Scottish pedlar. He also literally consumes nature: in the course of the journey he and his compatriots regularly hunt, taking advantage of the abundance and diversity of American mega fauna. They thus enjoy a sport that, in Britain at least, was largely the domain of the upper classes. Along the way, Wilson incorporates an explicit agenda calling for the domestication of the wilderness he traverses, and like Crevecoeur and Jefferson, extols agriculture as the most productive and virtuous way to interact with nature. Yet even as he promotes an agrarian agenda, he exhibits nostalgia for his version of the Romantic Indian's way of life.

The poem throughout demonstrates ambivalence about how a poet, particularly a poet whose social class is shifting as he heads deeper into the American wilderness, can and should interact with the natural environment and its inhabitants, which are both like and unlike what he left behind in Scotland. In this manner, the poem demonstrates a key feature of Romantic-period transatlanticism. Early American literature does not simply transpose its British influences; rather, as Giles notes, we see in poems like Wilson's 'how the emergence of separate political identities during this era can be seen as intertwined with a play of opposites, a series of reciprocal attractions and repulsions between opposing national situations'.[7] I want to elaborate on this play of opposites by discussing a few features of the poem, primarily its scenes of hunting, as well as the several episodes depicting the Native American peoples driven from the territory that Wilson traverses.

In her study *The Invention of the Countryside* Donna Landry describes how, during the period between 1671 and 1831, the activities of hunting and walking came to define what the English understood as 'the countryside' as an aesthetic idea essential to the formation of national identity. England's mythical 'green and pleasant land' was largely the creation of the hunters and walkers who, though often ideologically opposed to one another, both contributed to the conservation of rural spaces from agricultural or industrial development. As Landry amply demonstrates, hunting and walking were activities with explicit class markers, legible even today across England. In *The Foresters*, such activities are conducted simultaneously, by a former Scottish pedlar, and displaced to the wilds of western Pennsylvania. Hunting and walking organise the poem's narration and define the poet's relationship to the landscape and to his new nation.

Wilson is well aware of the discursive tradition that he is writing within and against. He had written a more traditional loco-descriptive poem while still in Scotland, *Lochwinnoch*, which was included in his first collection of 1790. As he claims in the final line of his invocation to *The Foresters*, he is taking up 'Scenes new to song, and paths untrod before'.[8] In this poem, from the outset, Wilson sees his work in opposition to the mainstream of British loco-descriptive poetry. He asks:

> To Europe's shores, renowned in deathless song,
> Must all the honours of the bard belong?
> And rural Poetry's enchanting strain
> Be only heard beyond th'Atlantic main? (17–20)

Wilson goes on to invoke other early American poets such as the Connecticut Wits David Humphreys and Joel Barlow and nature poet Philip Freneau. Yet, despite their accomplishments, the sublime American countryside remains uncelebrated, while the paltry English landscape is immortalised:

> Yet Nature's charms that bloom so lovely here
> Unhailed arrive, unheeded disappear;
> While bleak bare heaths, and brooks of half a mile
> Can rouse a thousand bards of Britain's Isle.
> There scarce a stream creeps down its narrow bed,
> There scarce a hillock lifts its little head,
> Or humble hamlet peeps their glades among,
> But lives and murmurs in immortal song. [...] (25–32)

By contrast, the 'vast transparent lakes and boundless woods ... Unhonoured weep the silent lapse of Time' (34, 36). For poets too, America is the land of opportunity. Wilson envisions himself originally celebrating the American countryside that, while sublime and picturesque like its British counterpart, offers a unique topography.

Even as the land provides virgin material for poetry, Wilson draws amply upon the conventions of old world poetry. He praises rural industry and hospitality in easily recognisable georgic terms. The prospect scenes he views from the various mountains and hills he ascends provide fodder for the requisite elevated meditations on the divine. Yet the poet's encounter with the birds and beasts signals some of the critical ecological and political distinctions between the American and British countryside. Even as he extols scenes of agricultural development, his attention in the poem is more often focused on hunting rather than farming. One is not likely to find in Jago or Dyer descriptions 'Of panthers trapt, of wounded bears enraged, / The wolves and wildcats he had oft engaged' (437–38). Dangerous wild animals, when they appear in English loco-descriptive poetry, are symbols of an otherness, whether of the distant past or of exotic settings, as we see in the early lines of *Windsor Forest*, for instance, when Pope describes how old England was 'a gloomy Waste, / To savage Beasts and Savage Laws a Prey'[9] or in Thomson's *Seasons,* where such animals are examples of the hazards of torrid climates. The absence of wolves and other such predators, both literal and figurative, is thus a hallmark of civilisation and temperate conditions. Yet in Wilson's poem, such animals are not necessarily an objective correlative of America's benighted condition or insalubrious environment. The poem, throughout, extols America's enlightened political and social vision coexisting with its abundance of wild animals and with the freedom afforded to hunt them.

Wilson's hunting is not only for the purposes of providing food for his journey, but also to defend himself against the very real threat of dangerous creatures lurking around every turn, as we see in the long passage describing his encounter with a rattlesnake. Startled and afraid, Wilson is prevailed upon by his travelling companion to spare the snake's life:

> 'O spare the brave!' our generous pilot cried,
> 'Let Mercy, sir! let Justice now decide;
> 'This noble foe, so terrible to sight,
> Though armed with death, yet ne'er provokes the fight. (687–90)

As his friend explains, the serpent merely responds to perceived threats when startled. The poem's praise for the snake and the peaceful outcome to the encounter of human and serpent suggest that America retains a prelapsarian perfection.

Other creatures fare less well, as the man who later made his fame as an ornithologist waxes eloquent about his large-scale slaughter of waterfowl. As abundant flocks of geese and ducks fly by:

> With sudden glance the smoky vengeance pour,
> And death and ruin spread along the shore
> The dead and dying mingling, float around,
> And loud the shoutings of my guides around. (1405–08)

This scene of carnage is interrupted by three stanzas describing the picturesque prospect around the lake and incorporating a hymn in praise of nature. Here the two modes of consuming nature are immediately juxtaposed, and Wilson goes back to describing his bounteous haul:

> There on the slaty shore, my spoils I spread,
> Ducks, plover, teal, the dying and the dead;
> Two snow-white storks, a crane of tawny hue,
> Stretched their long necks amid the slaughtered crew:
> A hawk, whose claws, white tail, and dappled breast,
> And eye, his royal pedigree confest;
> Snipes, splendid summer-ducks, and divers wild,
> In one high heap triumphantly I piled. (1445–52)

The travellers kill more birds than they can reasonably examine, eat, or even carry with them to eat later. America is a land of abundance, of nature's bounty, the land and the products of the land are democratically accessible to all classes and nationalities. Then as now, for Americans, this abundance has underwritten a wastefulness that Wilson's hunting scene exemplifies. While it would be anachronistic to project onto early nineteenth-century practices of natural history mainstream modern sensibilities regarding the needless killing of animals, Wilson himself does elsewhere display what Michael Branch identifies as an 'incipient ecological sensibility'. Branch narrates an incidence of Wilson's 'activism on behalf of birds' in 1807, when he attempted to stop the mass consumption of robins by sending an anonymous article to a Philadelphia newspaper falsely claiming that the robins' diet made them unfit for human consumption.[10]

Although Wilson is afforded many liberties in America, another group is denied the freedoms the poem elsewhere extols, namely the Native Americans whose dispossession and eradication provide the precondition of Wilson's freedom to roam. The Native Americans are present in Wilson's text, but present in their persistent absence. Wilson is one of the numerous white writers on either side of the Atlantic who contribute to an ongoing discourse about Indians and the value of their culture, and his work exhibits elements of both eighteenth-century and Romantic stereotypes. Wilson joins numerous other writers, particularly of Scottish origin, who take interest in American indigenous peoples. Several recent critical studies have drawn attention to the significant affinities between Scottish intellectuals and artists and Native American peoples, including most recently Colin G. Galloway in his *White People, Indians, and Highlanders: Tribal Peoples and Colonial Encounters in Scotland and America* (2008). Linda Colley has a useful account of British responses to Native Americans in her *Captives* (2002), and there are several relevant essays in *Native Americans and Anglo-American Culture, 1750–1850* (2009), edited by Tim Fulford and Kevin Hutchings.[11]

Among the earliest colonial authors of Scottish descent who wrote about the indigenous peoples of the northeastern region of North America was Cadwallader Colden, who served as the first colonial representative to the Iroquois nation and who wrote *The History of the Five Nations Depending on the Province of New York* (1727). Captain Robert Stobo, whose *Memoirs of Major R.S* (1800) were published posthumously, gave Tobias Smollett his model for what may be one of the more popular representations of the experience of Scottish adventurers in the colonies, namely that of Lieutenant Obadiah Lismahago, whose captivity narrative is included in Smollett's novel *The Expedition of Humphry Clinker* (1771). Smollett also provided details about Native Americans in his 'History of Canada' which appeared in the *British Magazine* (1760–64). In *Savages within the Empire: Representations of American Indians in Eighteenth-Century Britain*, Troy Bickham notes that, with rare exception, during the majority of the eighteenth century, representations of Native Americans were very much like those found in Wilson's poem, namely fairly 'generic'. The Indian of most literary representations 'could have been any primitive – accuracy of dress or tribal affiliation was unimportant'.[12] Bickham identifies John Shebbeare's novel *Lydia; or, Filial Piety* (1755) as one of the few variants to this pattern, claiming that 'So long as British battles with American Indians received detailed coverage in the British press, the image of the Indian had little chance of improving'.[13] However, by the early 1800s when Wilson was composing his work, this image had begun to shift in inverse proportion to the threat posed to British colonists.

According to Tim Fulford and Kevin Hutchings, in the Romantic period, 'Indians were now cycled and recycled as text from New York to London and back by white writers looking to romanticise their seeming disappearance. They thus blossomed as literary figures even as they were uprooted from their homelands'.[14] Early in the poem, for example, the travellers pass the site of the Battle of Wyoming, 'Where Indian rage prevailed, by murder fired, / And warriors brave by savage hand expired' (547–48). The poet surveys the scene where 'screams of horror pierced the midnight wood, / And the dire axe drank deep of human blood' (551–52). This same battle was depicted by Wilson's fellow Scot, Thomas Campbell, in *Gertrude of Wyoming* (1809; thus unlikely to have been a direct influence on Wilson's poem). Tim Fulford has recently written about the critical role that Native Americans played in the British fight against the American colonists. Whatever else might be said of such so-called 'Native savagery', for many Americans it was carried out in league with the British army, and as such, many at the time regarded the brutality against the American patriots as driven by English more than Iroquois interests.[15] Wilson's depiction of Indian viciousness may thus be read as a critique of England as much as of the first inhabitants of his new home, as well as an example of the eighteenth-century tropes commonly employed to depict Native Americans.

Native Americans appear elsewhere in the text but again through their traces on the land. In another key passage, the fate of native peoples is explicitly tied to European politics. Midway through the poem, Wilson describes a scene 'where late the skulking Indian trod, / Smeared with infant's and the mother's blood' (899–900). Although large-scale removal of the Native Americans from their land did not get underway until the presidency of Andrew Jackson in the 1830s, it was Thomas Jefferson (one of Wilson's patrons) who, at the time that Wilson was writing this poem, laid the groundwork for the large-scale dispossession that was to occur throughout the nineteenth century. Paradoxically, the land left by the Indians is settled by exiled French Royalists, to whom Wilson's poems wish peace and prosperity.

Memories of battles significant to the founding of the nation are key ingredients in English prospect poetry, as poems such as *Cooper's Hill* and *Edge-*

hill demonstrate. In depicting very recent battles involving Native Americans, Wilson complicates and subverts the movement of the *concordia discors* that such scenes typically underwrite. The struggles the poem inventories are quite recent and not quite resolved, as we see in the even more detailed description that Wilson offers of the Sullivan Expedition, which was the American army's response to the Battle of Wyoming. This campaign amounted to a virtual holocaust of the Iroquois nation in what is now upstate New York. (It was these events that led to George Washington being called in Iroquois 'Town Destroyer'.) For Wilson, because these Indians collaborated with the British, their eradication is a boon to be celebrated. Sullivan who 'scourged this crew' (1111) and who brought 'Fire, rapine and murder' (1104) is praised as a hero, and the land, cleansed of the 'bloody bands' (1103), is transformed into a new Eden:

> Where wretched wigwams late like kennels stood,
> Where bark-canoes stole skulking o'er the flood,
> Where mangled prisoners groaned, and hatchets glared,
> And blood-stained savages the fire prepared!
> There glittering towns and villages extend,
> There floating granaries in fleets descend,
> There ploughmen chant, and mowers sweep the soil,
> And taverns shine, and rosy damsels smile.
> Thanks to the brave, who through these forests bore
> Columbia's vengeance on the sons of gore;
> Who drove them howling through th' affrighted waste,
> Till British regions sheltered them at last. (1117–28)

The last line stresses the association of such savagery with Britain, thus the negative portrayal of the Native Americans is by implication a critique of the British. As Fulford has commented in his analysis of the literary representations of the Wyoming battle, narratives like Campbell's and Wilson's 'brought the Indian into uneasy relationship with Britons: they undermined his otherness as they suggested white men might be responsible for his "savagery". […] Employing Indians in its war undermined Britain's claims to be a civilised colonial power'.[16] Wilson's poem voices the political complexities of the newly founded nation, as a former colony that was already beginning to carve out its own empire through westward expansion.

Wilson's depiction of the Native Americans is not entirely negative, as we see in a subsequent nostalgic passage that provides a more sentimental soliloquy of a solitary Indian. Wilson's wandering Indian demonstrates many of what have come to be the stereotypical characteristics of what Fulford has defined as 'the

Romantic Indian', anticipated by figures like Cannasatego, the noble, naïve hero of *Lydia*. He is innocent and at one with nature, connected with his body but also experiencing a more 'extreme spirituality'.[17] In his commentary on this Indian's lament for his lost way of life, Wilson demonstrates a sympathy at odds with the portrayal of the British Indians in the passages describing battle scenes. He informs the reader, in case they needed the additional guidance, that 'A tear to Nature's tawny sons is due' (1328). Here he more explicitly argues what had been implicit in the earlier passages: 'The same false virtue and ambitious fire, / Which nations idolise and kings admire, / Provoke the white man to the bloody strife, / And bid the Indian to draw his deadly knife' (1329–32). The savagery of the savages is not innate but provoked by their colonisation.

Hunting is also associated with the Native Americans, and Wilson's depiction of them and their relationship to nature varies. On the one hand, they are depicted as savage and threatening, and their eradication from the landscape an unmitigated good for European settlers who are then safe to farm the land. On the other hand, the poet also demonstrates nostalgia for them and the simplicity of their way of life, in particular their lives as hunters, as we see in the passage describing the humble and virtuous life of the Indian Hunter near the poem's conclusion. He is apparently the only Native American actually present in the poem.

In *The Foresters*, the Scottish labouring-class poet turned 'first American ornithologist' and the Native American both stand in different ways as 'other' to English culture in North America. Their relationship to one another and to nature is more than a simple 'doubling'. Wilson is able to enjoy walking and hunting in the New World precisely because of the removal of the Native Americans. His freedom to roam and to hunt is simultaneously an appropriation of bourgeois and upper-class British modes of engaging the environment, but also emulates, in other ways, Native American practices of being in nature, even as it signals the disappearance and dispossession of the Indians. Although I have only begun to sketch some of the critical threads that might be unravelled, I would like to suggest that even this cursory analysis of Wilson's transatlantic poem provides provocative complications to the grand narratives of both American and British literary history and to the genre of nature writing in particular.

Notes

1   See, for example, John Barrell, *The Idea of Landscape and the Sense of Place, 1730–1840: An Approach to the Poetry of John Clare* (Cambridge: Cambridge University Press, 1972); David

Fairer, *English Poetry of the Eighteenth Century 1700–1789* (London: Longman, 2003); Tim Fulford, *Landscape, Liberty and Authority: Poetry, Criticism and Politics from Thomson to Wordsworth* (Cambridge: Cambridge University Press, 1996); John Goodridge, *Rural Life in Eighteenth-Century English Poetry* (Cambridge: Cambridge University Press, 1995); Donna Landry, *The Invention of the Countryside: Hunting, Walking, and Ecology in English Literature, 1671–1831* (Houndmills: Palgrave, 2001).

2   Timothy Fulford, *Romantic Indians: Native Americans, British Literature, & Transatlantic Culture 1756–1830* (Oxford: Oxford University Press, 2006); Paul Giles, *Atlantic Republic: The American Tradition in English Literature* (Oxford: Oxford University Press, 2006); Paul Giles, *Transatlantic Insurrections: British Culture and the Formation of American Literature, 1730–1860* (Philadelphia: University of Pennsylvania Press, 2001); Susan Manning, *Fragments of Union: Making Connections in Scottish and American Writing* (Houndmills: Palgrave, 2002); Susan Manning, *Transatlantic Literary Studies: A Reader* (Edinburgh: Edinburgh University Press, 2007); Lance Newman, *Our Common Dwelling: Henry Thoreau, Transcendentalism, and the Class Politics of Nature* (Houndmills: Palgrave, 2005); Joel Pace, 'Towards a Taxonomy of Transatlantic Romanticism(s)' *Literature Compass* 5, no. 2 (2008), 228–91; Lance Newman, Joel Pace and Christine Koenig-Woodyard (eds), *Sullen Fires Across the Atlantic: Essays in Transatlantic Romanticism*, Romantic Circles Praxis Series (November 2006), available online at http://romantic.arhu.umd.edu/praxis/sullenfires/ (accessed 7 July 2010).

3   Giles, *Transatlantic Insurrections,* 10–11.

4   Donna Landry, *The Muses of Resistance: Laboring-Class Women's Poetry in Britain, 1739–1796* (Cambridge: Cambridge University Press, 1990), 217–53.

5   Gary Harrison, 'Hybridity, Mimicry and John Clare's Child Harold', *The Wordsworth Circle* 34, no. 3 (2003): 149–55.

6   Laura Rigal, 'Empire of Birds: Alexander Wilson's American Ornithology', *The Huntington Library Quarterly* 59, nos 2–3 (1996): 223–68.

7   Giles, *Transatlantic Insurrections,* 1.

8   Alexander Wilson, *The Poems and Literary Prose of Alexander Wilson*, vol. II (Paisley, 1876), 157, line 16. All subsequent selections from the poem will be taken from this edition with line numbers provided in the text.

9   Alexander Pope, 'Windsor Forest' in *Eighteenth-Century Poetry,* ed. David Fairer and Christine Gerrard (Oxford: Blackwell, 1999), lines 44–45.

10 Michael Branch, 'Indexing American Possibilities: The Natural History Writing of Bartram, Wilson and Audubon' in *The Ecocriticism Reader,* ed. Cheryll Glotfelty and Harold Fromm (Athens, GA: The University of Georgia Press, 1996), 291–92.

11 Colin G. Calloway, *White People, Indians, and Highlanders: Tribal Peoples and Colonial Encounters in Scotland and America* (New York: Oxford University Press, 2008); Linda Colley, *Captives: Britain, Empire and the World 1600–1850* (London: Cape, 2002); *Native Americans and Anglo-American Culture, 1750–1850: The Indian Atlantic,* ed. Tim Fulford and Kevin Hutchings (Cambridge: Cambridge University Press, 2009).

12 Troy Bickham, *Savages within the Empire: Representations of American Indians in Eighteenth-Century Britain* (Oxford: Oxford University Press, 2006), 96.

13 Bickham, *Savages within the Empire*, 96.

14 Tim Fulford and Kevin Hutchings (eds), *Native Americans and Anglo-American Culture*, 5.

15 Tim Fulford, 'Romantic Indians and Colonial Politics: The Case of Thomas Campbell', *Symbiosis* 2, no. 2 (1998), 203–23.

16 Fulford, 'Romantic Indians and Colonial Politics', 211.

17 Fulford, 'Romantic Indians and Colonial Politics', 209.

'Tracing the Ramifications of the Democratic Principle': Literary Criticism and Theory in the *Chartist Circular*

Mike Sanders

The regular appearance of both literary criticism and literary theory in Chartist journals did not represent a new departure in the practice of working-class radical journalism. As Paul Murphy has shown in *Toward a Working-Class Canon*, a tradition of working-class literary criticism, frequently engaging with the 'canon' can be traced back at least as far as 1816. The history of working-class literary criticism in the first half of the nineteenth century, Murphy argues, is one of a general broadening of attitudes from a sceptical, suspicious and, at times, openly hostile approach to literature (exemplified by Richard Carlile and William Cobbett) to a more generous recognition of the political importance of the 'aesthetic'. During the 1840s and '50s, Murphy notes, many Chartist writers attested to their belief in 'the inseparable interconnection of the beautiful, the imaginative, and the truthful in literature and in the minds of readers'.[1] Murphy also identifies a process of canon formation with 'working-class journalists disestablishing and recanonizing established writers, or sanctioning new, unestablished writers, to fit the values of their own class.'[2]

This article is, in part, a response to Murphy's work and it takes the form of a detailed analysis of the *Chartist Circular*, a weekly journal printed in Glasgow and published under the superintendence of the Universal Suffrage Central Committee for Scotland (USCCS). In particular, this article will engage both with Chartist literary criticism and Chartist literary theory by concentrating on three interconnected issues: the creation of a Chartist canon through the excavation of a Chartist literary heritage; the creation of an anti-Chartist literary heritage; and an analysis of the general social and political role played by poetry.

The *Chartist Circular* ran for 146 issues from 28th September 1839 to 9th July 1842 (when debts forced its closure). Its editor, William Thomson, also served as general secretary to the USCCS. Thomson had previously served as secretary to the Scottish National Association for the Protection of Hand-loom Weavers and had edited the *Weavers' Journal* from October 1835 to April 1837. In addition to his trade union and Chartist activities, Thomson was a co-operator and a key figure in the Total Abstinence movement (serving as president of the Scottish Total Abstinence Society). Following the closure of the *Chartist Circular*, Thomson left the Chartist movement and joined the Complete Suffrage Movement.[3]

The life-span of the *Chartist Circular* coincided with an important period in Chartist history; it began publishing some five weeks before the Newport Uprising and ceased some two months after the presentation of the second Chartist petition and just over a month before the mass industrial unrest of August–September 1842. It cost a halfpenny and consisted of four pages. Unlike the *Northern Star* it was not a newspaper: W. Hamish Fraser describes it as 'an educational journal intended to bring a greater understanding of the aims of Chartism'.[4] Its front page consisted of an original editorial while the rest of the journal offered a combination of longer articles on political, economic and social matters, shorter miscellaneous articles of an improving nature, brief extracts from a range of radical writers, humorous stories with a political/satirical edge, as well as original poetry and fiction.[5] Early issues are evenly divided between original and reprinted material, but from around number fifteen the volume of original material rises to three-quarters of each issue. Except for the poetry column, most of the original material is unattributed and is, presumably, the work of the journal's editor.[6] At its peak it enjoyed a circulation in excess of 20,000 copies and played a key role in organising Scottish Chartism at a national level. Like much of Scottish Chartism it inclined to 'moral' rather than 'physical' force – a position influenced by the memory of the Scottish insurrection of 1820 (whose aftermath saw three hangings, sixteen transportations and numerous imprisonments).[7]

The *Chartist Circular* published a great deal of poetry: most editions carried an original poetry column and in the political and editorial articles, poetry was frequently quoted in support of an argument. However, the construction of a Chartist canon occurred through two series, 'The Politics of Poets' and 'Literary Sketches', neither of which has an identified (or identifiable) author. 'The Politics of Poets' ran for ten numbers from 11th July 1840 to 13th March 1841; it briefly overlapped with 'Literary Sketches' which ran for 29 numbers from 13th February 1841 to 9th April 1842. The relatively late appearance of these series requires comment. 'The Politics of Poets' begins in no. 42, whereas the poetry column itself had appeared on an almost weekly basis from no. 3 onwards. Thus, whilst original Chartist poetry is published almost from the *Chartist Circular*'s inception, it is almost a year before it begins to analyse and discuss poetry. Priority is clearly given to encouraging Chartist poetic production ahead of 'canonical engagement' and this follows the editorial policy pursued in the *Northern Star* at the same period. Yet, we might ask what prompts the move into literary criticism?

Firstly, I want to anticipate and discard the sceptical argument which would regard these literary articles merely as 'space-fillers'. The size, location and extent of both series – both published on the second page of each number (i.e. immediately after the front page editorial) with individual articles frequently running to two and even three columns (3 columns = 1 page) and with the series extending over many numbers – demonstrates that this was more than an editorial afterthought. It is interesting to note that the increasing importance of poetry in the *Chartist Circular* occurs in parallel with a very similar process in the *Northern Star*. As I have demonstrated in *The Poetry of Chartism*, between June and September 1840 the poetry column 'moves, both literally and symbolically, from the margins to the ideological centre of the *Northern Star*'.[8] Two articles published prior to 'The Politics of Poets' series provide a clue as to why the Chartist movement was beginning to attribute such importance to poetry. The sixth number of the *Chartist Circular*, published 2nd November 1839, contains an article entitled 'Morality of the Working Classes' written as a response to *Blackwood's Magazine*'s claim that the working classes are currently 'too ignorant, too drunk and improvident' to be trusted with the franchise. The *Chartist Circular* responds to this by citing the drive to self-education in working-class communities as evidence of the intellectual and moral abilities of the working classes, and by lambasting the government for failing to provide the working classes with meaningful educational opportunities.[9] In short, in the words of Fraser, '[t]he *Circular*'s argument was that the working class was *already* morally and intellectually worthy of the vote.'[10]

Some months later, 9th May 1840, in an article entitled 'The Genius of Working Men', the *Chartist Circular* claims that 'natural genius […] is indigenous and belongs almost exclusively to working men. In every village we find an untaught poet, a painter, a musician […]'. Indeed, the writer claims that natural genius '*belong*[s] *almost exclusively to the working masses*' and cites, amongst others, Homer, Æsop, Socrates, Milton, Shakespeare, Burns, Tannahill and Bloomfield in support of this claim, before concluding, 'There is, therefore, no deficiency of *intellect* among the poor'.[11] Taken together, these articles assert that the knowledge, intellect, literary judgement and creativity already displayed by the working classes, demonstrates their inherent fitness to exercise the franchise. Elsewhere I have described this proposition as 'the argument from culture' and have suggested that it performed a key role in Chartist strategic thinking in the interval between the rejection of the second petition and the emergence of the Chartist Land Plan.[12] In this respect, the dates of these articles are significant: 'The Morality of the Working Classes' appears just days before the Newport Uprising exposed the limitations of an insurrectionary strategy, whilst the two series occupy the period before the second Chartist petition. The *Chartist Circular* is making the 'argument from culture' some three years in advance of the *Northern Star* (which starts to deploy this argument from 1844 onwards).

'The Politics of Poets' begins with Ebenezer Elliott's rejection of those critics who are already seeking to de-politicise the canon:

> The gentleman critics complain that the union of poetry and politics is always hurtful to the politics, and fatal to the poetry. But these great connoisseurs must be wrong, if Homer, Dante, Shakespeare, Milton, Cowper, and Burns were poets.[13]

Rather the *Chartist Circular* identifies poetry with politics – 'All genuine poets are fervid politicians'; poetry is defined as 'impassioned truth', and in an almost Blakean aphorism the article declares 'All truth is radical'. The article strikes a recognisably Shelleyan note in its insistence that poets constitute the vanguard of humanity, proclaiming the truth of liberty in advance of its political realisation. Noting that 'Poets and their poetry have, and will continue to exert an extensive influence on the destinies of mankind', the *Chartist Circular* declares that its intention in 'The Politics of Poets' series: 'is to take an advantage of this great inherent power in our national poetry that we propose to bring before our readers the leading political principles developed in their writings'.[14]

The articles which follow focus initially on the Romantic poets – Shelley, Byron, Wordsworth, Coleridge and the young Southey, are all discussed and praised for their republican/democratic tendencies.

The sixth number of 'The Politics of Poets', however, turns its attention to what it describes as contemporary 'minor poets' (by which it appears to mean working-class poets). This article begins with the claim that 'Almost every town, village, and hamlet in Scotland has its poet, whose song in his own locality is listened to with feeling and respect'.[15] Although obscure in their lifetimes and forgotten after death these local poets too are 'unacknowledged legislators' in so far as 'the influence of [their] talents can never be wholly lost to society'. The decision to look at contemporary working-class writers is justified on political rather than aesthetic grounds. Indeed, despite its earlier claims of an abundance of natural genius amongst the working classes, only one column in the series is dedicated to a single working-class poet. Samuel Bamford's poetry is discussed in the ninth number of 'The Politics of Poets' (no. 67, 2nd January 1841), and some indication of the precarious transmission of the working-class literary tradition is given by the column's report that Bamford had died in the battle of Orthes. (This report is corrected four numbers later, where Bamford's account of Peterloo taken from his forthcoming *Passages in the Life of a Radical* is also published.)

In its discussion of contemporary working-class poets, the *Chartist Circular* makes it clear that its interest lies in the extent to which such poets represent 'the state of popular feeling'.[16] Furthermore, it argues, 'It matters, little, however rude the strain; like the feather it tells the way the wind blows.' The article claims that an ancient love of song and an independent spirit has generated an unquenchable desire for liberty amongst the Scottish people. The interchange between politics and poetry is understood as a two-way process. Poetry inspires and sustains political activity:

> Poetry is a lever of commanding influence when it grasps the subject that interests, or the elements that move the popular will. It penetrates to every nerve and fibre of society, stirring into irresistibility its undermost current […][17]

However, political activity also exerts a pressure on poetic expression. The *Chartist Circular* argues that the ongoing struggle for popular rights has 'conveyed a corresponding spirit to our poetry, giving it a more intense and earnest feeling for the cause'. It then situates this change in a broader historical context arguing that:

> Ever since the French Revolution mere sentiment in poetry has been giving way for that of principle – high, unbending principle […] despotism deepens its gloom; the lights of fancy alone are inadequate to struggle with its darkness. Poetry needed, and received, a higher and a firmer tone; if it has lost in feeling, it has gained in power.[18]

I will return to poetry's role in enabling such a 'politics of feeling' later in this article. For the moment, I want to consider a different account of poetry offered by an article published in the same edition of the *Chartist Circular*.

Entitled 'Literary Reform', this article begins, 'I do not know anything more essential for the improvement of mankind […] than a Radical Literary Reform'. This sounds a very different note from previous discussions, as it focuses on literature as an instrument of oppression rather than liberation. The central accusation is that literature has glorified and glamorised the actions of princes and heroes such that 'their selfishness, murders, battles, and massacres, have been falsely extolled for valour, magnanimity, and patriotism'. In a moment of Benjaminian insight, the article highlights a structural link between the actual violence perpetrated by class societies and the symbolic violence which underpins their modes of aesthetic representation:

> History does not condescend to extol the virtuous poor: it only venerates kings, priests, and generals […] Poetry and romance delight to decorate the nobility […] The poetry of humble life is not fashionable; a romance of cottagers would be a tale of nasty creatures which nobody would write, and few read.[19]

It notes that lower-class characters only appear as either 'base and ignoble' or 'servile and sensual', and if a 'lower-class' hero ever demonstrates real virtue then you may be sure that their aristocratic origins will be quickly discovered. This analysis combines a rudimentary 'politics of narrative' with an understanding of the role of ideological misrecognition in securing the hegemonic effectiveness of literature. The result of this 'false philosophy' promulgated by 'literary authors' is that 'the masses, in ignorance, have worshipped their oppressors, as if they were incarnate divinities. So long as this literary vileness continues, so long will the people be led astray.' The remedy for this state of affairs is a 'Radical Literary Reform' which will extol the 'virtues of the masses' and expose and condemn 'the iniquities of the *titled*', and for the people to 'read only those good works which do them justice'.

Two weeks after the 'Literary Reform' article the *Chartist Circular* starts a new series entitled 'Literary Sketches' which quickly replaces 'The Politics of Poets' series. 'Literary Sketches' runs for almost three times as long as 'The Politics of Poets' and is a far more ambitious series in terms of its range and scope. It moves beyond the Romantics to discuss Milton, Henryson, Cowper and Goldsmith, it deals with a range of working-class poets from the better-known such as Tannahill and Bloomfield to more obscure Glasgow poets such as Walter Currie, Thomas Gillespie and Tom Atkenson. This series also examines some American poets and discusses a number of important historical figures such as John Knox and James I and James V of Scotland.

On one level 'Literary Sketches' like 'The Politics of Poets' can be understood as an attempt to construct a 'national-popular' cultural tradition. Thus James I is described as 'the literary royal radical of Scotland [...] assassinated by his rebellious nobles for being a political reformer' and the article concludes by calling on its readers to 'honour his virtues, venerate his politics, embalm and love his memory, read his poetry, [and] sing his music'.[20] Similarly, Robert Henryson (the fifteenth-century poet) is praised for having 'the bold sentiments of a Radical Reformer' although in an interesting recognition of historical difference the *Chartist Circular* notes that in the fifteenth century political notions were expressed by means of religious aspirations.[21] Similarly, John Knox is claimed as 'a zealous Radical Reformer – a Democrat – a Republican, and a physical-force Chartist.'[22]

However, 'Literary Sketches' goes beyond 'The Politics of Poets' in three crucial respects. Firstly, it pays much greater attention to those it describes as the 'unknown poets of the people'.[23] Secondly, 'Literary Sketches' explicitly recognises that poetry is a contested tradition and this is particularly evident in its treatment of Burns and Byron. The *Chartist Circular* finds it necessary to claim Burns as:

a republican, a democrat; and in principle and practice, an honest Chartist. Ye who sneer at this assertion, read his 'Man was made to Mourn', 'A Man's a Man for a' that', 'The Twa Dogs', and 'A Winter Night', and your Whiggish doubts will vanish like the hoary mountain mist before the bright rays of the meridian summer sun.[24]

In the case of Byron the *Chartist Circular* makes it clear that it is necessary to retrieve his reputation from 'the malicious falsehoods with which ecclesiastical hypocrisy and political iniquity have dared to malign [his] honest intentions and noble character'.[25]

Thirdly, and arguably most importantly, 'Literary Sketches' engages with writers and poets whom it considers to be hostile to Chartist values, most notably Walter Scott, Allan Ramsay and John Home. Thus the *Chartist Circular* can be seen as creating an anti-Chartist canon. Walter Scott, who is the subject of the very first 'Literary Sketch', is criticised for the perceived political tendencies of his work:

> The subtle effect of his great historical panoramas is, to exalt the aristocracy, and debase the people; to excite veneration for Chiefs and Ladies, and contempt for the masses […] He throws a false gloss over the political and social misery of […] feudalism.[26]

It is the content and political implications of Scott's work that the *Chartist Circular* objects to, it does not dispute his skill as a writer:

> Sir Walter Scott is a popular author of great genius […] But as he has written too much for the benefit of the oppressors, and the obloquy of the oppressed, we gaze on his mighty enchantments with the painful emotions of pity and gloom […].[27]

The *Circular*'s major anxiety is that Scott's success in aestheticising feudalism will inculcate hostility to the 'democratic voice':

> The fascinating perusal of his popular works, in our early days, makes very false impressions on our youthful minds, and in manhood causes us to linger among the ruins of the past, and makes us shudder when we hear the democratic voice of the people rejoicing over feudal decay, and extolling, with laudable gladness, the march of equality among the human race.[28]

However, the article concludes by claiming that after 'Literary Reform' has occurred, the taste for Scott's works will decline:

> When the people shall have their own authors and press, to do them justice, they will sweep away the corruptions of literature from the haunts of social life, and the proud motto of Knowledge and Equality shall then wave triumphantly on the noble banner of Literary Reform.[29]

The *Chartist Circular*'s anxiety concerning Scott's influence appears to have been well-placed. Jonathan Rose's pioneering study, *The Intellectual Life of the British Working Classes*, notes that the Dunfermline weavers 'were clubbing together to buy the Waverley novels'.[30] (Such activity might well have come to Thomson's attention in his previous position as secretary to the Scottish weavers' union). Of particular concern to the *Chartist Circular* is the political effect of imaginative literature on young minds. Some of Scott's 'delusive romances' are, in the opinion of the *Chartist Circular*, 'unfit to be read by the junior masses, before their minds are matured with the knowledge of sound philosophy and political truth'. The subsequent discussion of Allan Ramsay's work identifies some of the *Chartist Circular*'s concerns. Ramsay's work, especially his *Gentle Shepherd*, is criticised not just for its 'unmanly adulation of the *titled* great' and its 'unmerited degradation of their vassals' or what the *Chartist Circular* succinctly describes as its 'people-debasing politics'. The *Chartist Circular* also regrets the gaps in Ramsay's poem which, in spite of being set around the time of the English Revolution, 'contains no holy aspirations for civil and religious liberty, although the scene is laid at a time in Scottish history when the people were boldly struggling for their rights'. However, the principal objection to Ramsay's work lies in its capacity (particularly in the educational field) to inculcate 'Tory' values by stealth:

> When I was at school, the Gentle Shepherd, and the tragedy of Douglas, were read as schoolbooks, by the scholars. I did not then comprehend their political tendency, and the master never explained it. I admired Patie and Douglas, and thought them gallant and noble; the vassals I laughed at and despised.
>
> Thus was the intention of the teacher of Toryism fulfilled, – the minds of his pupils were poisoned with false political principles, and the seeds of Toryism were sown, which, like weeds in the garden, can never again be entirely eradicated from the soil.[31]

The central political objection to Scott, Ramsay and Home is that through a process of emotional identification with a character, the values of Toryism are unknowingly internalised and possess greater political effect precisely because of this – as Althusser noted, the successful ideology never proclaims 'I am ideological'.

In offering such a critique, the *Chartist Circular* clearly regards Scott's novels as performing 'ideological work' (to use an anachronistic term from modern literary theory). Recently, this notion of textual agency has been powerfully challenged by Jonathan Rose, who argues:

> It is meaningless, then, to speak of the 'ideological work' performed by Scripture or any other text. Texts do nothing by themselves. The work is performed by the reader, using the text as a tool.[32]

In a section entitled 'Conservative Authors and Radical Readers', Rose shows how working-class readers were able to produce politically radical interpretations of a range of conservative authors including Scott.[33] Indeed, there is a sense in which Rose deploys Scott as his test case, commenting that early nineteenth-century radical papers 'often assailed Walter Scott's conservatism, but their readers did not necessarily concur'.[34] However, the overwhelming majority of Rose's examples of radical re-evaluations of Scott are drawn from readers born in the post-Chartist period (from 1860 onwards), which suggests that this particular strategy was not so readily available to Chartist readers. During this period it would seem that the 'intended' ideological pressures of the text were more difficult to resist and/or redirect than they were for subsequent generations of working-class readers.

In part, this might be due to the close association between emotional affect and political effect which remains a constant in the *Chartist Circular*'s literary theory. For when we move from the critique of anti-Chartist poetry to a consideration of the positive role which poetry can play in the struggle for democratic rights, we find a similar emphasis placed on the multi-vocal yet essentially emotional nature of poetry:

> The voices are many by which poetry speaks. At one time it appeals to all the soft and gentle feelings of our nature – at another it swells the heart with indignation against the ruthless oppressors of our species. At another time it speaks in the bold prophetic language of truth, singing of the increasing power and strength of the people [...] Again it utters wrathful thundering against the proud and ambitious, who drench the earth in blood, and clothe the world with ruin, for the paltry purpose of winning a crown – anon it sings the jubilee hymn of freedom.[35]

The poet chosen to exemplify this aspect of poetry is Lord Byron. The *Chartist Circular* contrasts Byron's interest in humankind with the inward focus of some of his contemporaries and in so doing identifies a new social task for poetry which it describes as 'tracing through its ramified complications the development of the democratic principle which the minds of men, in the different nations of the world, had so largely imbibed, at and subsequent to the [French] Revolution'.[36]

In conclusion then, the *Chartist Circular* offers two forms of canonical engagement: the construction of a literary canon which is also the embodiment of a 'national-popular' democratic tradition, and the identification of an opposing canon which is hostile to democratic values. The *Chartist Circular* identifies working-class poetic production with the first tradition thereby making working-class poetry continuous with and not a radical departure from established poetic forms and conventions.

Notes

1   Paul Thomas Murphy, *Toward a Working-Class Canon: Literary Criticism in British Working-Class Periodicals, 1816–1858* (Ohio: Ohio State University Press, 1994), 58.
2   Murphy, *Toward a Working-Class Canon*, 3.
3   For details of Thomson's career, see Alexander Wilson, *The Chartist Movement in Scotland* (Manchester: Manchester University Press, 1970), 80–81, 131–35, 182–84, 195–96. For details of the relationship between Chartism and the Complete Suffrage Movement see Malcolm Chase, *Chartism: A New History* (Manchester: Manchester University Press, 2007), 198–238.
4   W. Hamish Fraser, 'The Chartist Press in Scotland', in *Papers for the People: A Study of the Chartist Press*, eds Joan Allen and Owen R. Ashton (London: Merlin Press, 2005), 91.
5   A brief digest of no. 74 (20 February 1841) offers a representative sample of the *Chartist Circular*'s contents; front page editorial, 'The Possession of Popular Rights the Elements of a Nation's Power', longer articles on 'Robert Burns', 'Casanova's Flight from the Lead-Chambers at Venice', 'Thoughts on the Dungeon, on the French Revolution', 'Political Catechism: On the Suffrage', 'Patriotism', the Poetry Column and a number of shorter miscellaneous articles on the Rev. Rowland Hill, the Bank of England, Catherine I of Russia, Second-hand Sermons and a brief extract from Wollstonecraft.
6   Some of the *Chartist Circular*'s original material is attributed. Fraser, for example, notes that in its 'early issues, Alexander Purdie, the chair of the Glasgow Universal Suffrage Association, discussed each of the Six Points [of the People's Charter] in turn'. W. Hamish Fraser, 'The Chartist Press in Scotland', 91–92.
7   Fraser, 'The Chartist Press in Scotland', provides a helpful overview of the debate between 'moral' and 'physical' force Chartism in the Scottish Chartist press.
8   Mike Sanders, *The Poetry of Chartism: Aesthetics, Politics, History* (Cambridge: Cambridge University Press, 2009), 73.
9   'Morality of the Working Classes', *Chartist Circular*, no. 6 (2 November 1839), 22.
10 Fraser, 'The Chartist Press in Scotland', 93.
11 'The Genius of Working Men', *Chartist Circular*, no. 33 (9 May 1840), 135–36.
12 Sanders, *The Poetry of Chartism*, 76–77, 85.
13 'The Politics of Poets. No. 1', *Chartist Circular*, no. 42 (11 July 1840), 170.
14 'The Politics of Poets. No. 1', *Chartist Circular*, no. 42 (11 July 1840), 170.
15 'The Politics of Poets. No. 6', *Chartist Circular*, no. 57 (24 October 1840), 231.
16 'The Politics of Poets. No. 6', *Chartist Circular*, no. 57 (24 October 1840), 231.

17 'The Politics of Poets. No. 6', *Chartist Circular*, no. 57 (24 October 1840), 231.
18 'The Politics of Poets. No. 6', *Chartist Circular*, no. 57 (24 October 1840), 231.
19 'Literary Reform', *Chartist Circular*, no. 71 (31 January 1841), 299.
20 'Literary Sketches, James I of Scotland', *Chartist Circular*, no. 94 (10 July 1841), 394.
21 'Literary Sketches, Robert Henryson', *Chartist Circular*, no. 90 (12 June 1841), 378.
22 'Literary Sketches, John Knox', *Chartist Circular*, no. 80 (3 April 1841), 338.
23 See, for example, 'Literary Sketches, devoted to poets of the people: Bloomfield, Allen, Rogers, Struthers', *Chartist Circular*, no. 101 (28 August 1841), 422; 'Literary Sketches, the unknown poets of the people', *Chartist Circular*, no. 108 (16 October 1841), 449–50.
24 'Literary Sketches, Robert Burns', *Chartist Circular*, no. 74 (20 February 1841), 309–10.
25 'Literary Sketches, Byron', *Chartist Circular*, no. 114 (27 November 1841), 473–74.
26 'Literary Sketches, Walter Scott', *Chartist Circular*, no. 73 (13 February 1841), 305–6.
27 'Literary Sketches, Walter Scott', *Chartist Circular*, no. 73 (13 February 1841), 305–6.
28 'Literary Sketches, Walter Scott', *Chartist Circular*, no. 73 (13 February 1841), 305–6.
29 'Literary Sketches, Walter Scott', *Chartist Circular*, no. 73 (13 February 1841), 305–6.
30 Jonathan Rose, *The Intellectual Life of the British Working Classes* (New Haven, CT: Yale University Press, 2001), 116.
31 'Literary Sketches, Allan Ramsay', *Chartist Circular*, no. 75 (27 February 1841), 314.
32 Rose, *The Intellectual Life of the British Working Classes*, 15
33 Rose, *The Intellectual Life of the British Working Classes*, 39–48.
34 Rose, *The Intellectual Life of the British Working Classes*, 40–41.
35 'Politics of Poets. No. VIII', *Chartist Circular*, no. 65 (19 December 1840), 265.
36 'Politics of Poets. No. VIII', *Chartist Circular*, no. 65 (19 December 1840), 265.

Labour History by Other Means
Jonathan Rose

A few years ago some labour historians at an English university confided to me that, when *The Intellectual Life of the British Working Classes*[1] was reviewed in the newspapers, they posted those reviews on their departmental bulletin board. As they explained it, the fact that an academic study of labour history could still attract the attention of the national press did wonders for their morale, which sorely needed boosting. True, their field had enjoyed a vogue for about twenty years, starting with E.P. Thompson's *The Making of the English Working Class* in 1963.[2] But it was gradually eclipsed by the historiography of gender and race, and in 1983 Gareth Stedman Jones's *Languages of Class: Studies in English Working Class History, 1832–1982* sent younger scholars off in yet another direction, exploring linguistics and culture.[3]

To be congratulated for revalidating working-class history was, for me, as ironic as it was gratifying, for I could hardly call myself a labour historian. Yes, as an American undergraduate and graduate student in the 1970s, I had been exposed to British labour history. My professors had assigned *The Making of the English Working Class*: whether I read it all the way to the end is another question. But my chosen specialty was intellectual history: while others of my generation were studying the workplace, trade unions, family structure, diet, housing, and wages, I much preferred the world of ideas. Naturally, I had to defend that peculiar taste in the classroom. Wasn't intellectual history elitist? Did the conversations of great minds have any real influence outside their own select circle? Shouldn't history be about everyday life, material culture, and the 'inarticulate masses'?

These were tough but fair questions, and ultimately I, along with many other intellectual historians, realised that they could only be answered by inventing a new academic field. It became known as 'the history of the book', an umbrella term broadly covering the social, economic, and cultural history of authorship, publishing, libraries, censorship, and reading. *The Intellectual Life of the British Working Classes* was very much a product of this movement. I found my models not in E.P. Thompson, but in Richard Altick's *The English Common Reader* and David Vincent's *Bread, Knowledge and Freedom*.[4] Book historians have never been solely concerned with the lower classes, but they have proven beyond a reasonable doubt that the great books had plebeian readers, that reading has long been a necessity of everyday life for ordinary people, that books were an important part of the material culture of most working-class homes, and that the 'inarticulate masses' produced a vast body of literature. Book history, then, offers at least two ideal vehicles for studying labouring-class culture.

The most obvious method is the historiography of reading, deployed not only in my book but also in several other works all published within a few years of each other: Christine Pawley's *Reading on the Middle Border: The Culture of Print in Late-Nineteenth-Century Osage, Iowa* (2001), Martyn Lyons's *Readers and Society in Nineteenth-Century France: Workers, Women, Peasants* (2001), Elizabeth McHenry's *Forgotten Readers: Recovering the Lost History of African American Literary Societies* (2002), and Thomas Augst's *The Clerk's Tale: Young Men and Moral Life in Nineteenth-Century America* (2003).[5] We all knew each other. We all were active in the Society for the History of Authorship, Reading and Publishing (SHARP), the international organisation of book historians. And we all used similar kinds of sources: mainly memoirs, library registers, and the records of mutual improvement societies.

Beyond that, researchers have recently developed two new valuable electronic resources for this field. At latest count, the Reading Experience Database (www.open.ac.uk/Arts/reading/) records 17,000 encounters with books by British subjects from 1450 to 1945. The soon-to-be-launched What Middletown Read Project (www.bsu.edu/middletown/wmr/) has compiled nearly every public library transaction between 1891 and 1902 in that quintessentially 'typical' American town, Muncie, Indiana – a total of more than 6,000 patrons, 13,000 volumes, and 400,000 loans. And both of these databases are searchable by class and occupation. Together with the Database of British and Irish Labouring-Class Poets at Nottingham Trent University (http://human.ntu.ac.uk/research/labouringclasswriters/DatabaseOfWriters.htm), these resources will enable us to study, with unprecedented precision and thoroughness, the literary lives of working people.

A second route for re-entering labour history is laid out by the Labouring-Class Writers Project itself: that is, the history of authorship. Along with Richard Altick and David Vincent, I also drew inspiration from Martha Vicinus's *The Industrial Muse* (1974).[6] Her book and the Database open up new scholarly frontiers, though we should bear in mind that not all working-class writers were obscure impoverished milltown versifiers. Quite a few of them, especially in the first half of the twentieth century, were successful well-known prose writers. If they have since fallen into a historiographical black hole, it is largely because they worked in a literary genre that academia despises and ignores. I don't mean lowbrow literature: there is no shortage of monographs on penny dreadfuls, pulp fiction, and pornography. No, what has been shamefully neglected is middlebrow literature. While highbrow culture was controlled by the guild of Bloomsbury, the middlebrow remained an open marketplace where working-class writers could address working-class readers, for example Howard Spring's *Fame is the Spur* (1940).[7] When I was writing my book I sensed the importance of Howard Spring and Ethel Mannin and

Alexander Baron, but I was not able to say much about them, simply because they had not yet generated a corpus of scholarly biographies and critical studies. Today the *MLA International Bibliography* lists just two hits for Spring, six for Mannin, and none for Baron, compared with 4,547 for Virginia Woolf. Woolf and F.R. Leavis pronounced that middlebrow authors were not worth reading, and generations of academics agreed. Not until the 1990s was that taboo finally broken, by Joan Shelley Rubin's *The Making of Middlebrow Culture, 1920–1950* (1992) and Rosa Maria Bracco's *'Betwixt and Between': Middlebrow Fiction and English Society in the Twenties and Thirties* (1990).[8] Rather than produce yet more books about Bloomsbury, we really need studies of the writers that the Bloomsberries defined themselves against, such as Christopher Hilliard's *To Exercise Our Talents: The Democratization of Writing in Britain* (2006).[9] We need to discover how these plebeian writers scrambled out of poverty up the ladder of popular journalism, how they transformed their life experiences into literature, how they appealed to working-class audiences. For the young labour historian – and the young critic of labour literature – a lifetime of important work remains to be done.

Notes

1 Jonathan Rose, *The Intellectual Life of the British Working Classes* (New Haven, CT: Yale University Press, 2001).

2 E.P. Thompson, *The Making of the English Working Class* (London: Gollancz, 1963).

3 Gareth Stedman Jones, *Languages of Class: Studies in English Working Class History, 1832–1982* (Cambridge: Cambridge University Press, 1983).

4 Richard Altick, *The English Common Reader: A Social History of the Mass Reading Public, 1800–1900* (Chicago: University of Chicago Press, 1957); David Vincent, *Bread, Knowledge and Freedom: A Study of Nineteenth-Century Working Class Autobiography* (London and New York: Methuen, 1981).

5 Christine Pawley, *Reading on the Middle Border: The Culture of Print in Late-Nineteenth-Century Osage, Iowa* (Amherst: University of Massachusetts, 2001); Martyn Lyons, *Readers and Society in Nineteenth-Century France: Workers, Women, Peasants* (Houndsmill: Palgrave, 2001); Elizabeth McHenry, *Forgotten Readers: Recovering the Lost History of African American Literary Societies* (Durham, NC: Duke University Press, 2002); Thomas Augst, The *Clerk's Tale: Young Men and Moral Life in Nineteenth-Century America* (Chicago: University of Chicago Press, 2003).

6 Martha Vicinus, *The Industrial Muse* (London: Croom Helm, 1974).

7 Howard Spring, *Fame is the Spur* (London: Collins, 1940).

8 Joan Shelley Rubin, *The Making of Middlebrow Culture, 1920–1950* (Chapel Hill and London: University of North Carolina Press, 1992); Rosa Maria Bracco, *'Betwixt and Between': Middlebrow Fiction and English Society in the Twenties and Thirties* (Parkville, Vic.: The University of Melbourne, 1990).

9 Christopher Hilliard, *To Exercise Our Talents: The Democratization of Writing in Britain* (Cambridge, MA and London: Harvard University Press, 2006).

Graphic Bric-a-brac: Comic Visual Culture and the Study of Early Victorian Lower-Class Urban Culture
Brian Maidment

In an issue of a journal devoted to the recovery and recuperation of various resources for the study of labouring-class history, visual culture from the first half of the nineteenth century offers something of a problem. Little visual culture from this period originated within the 'working class' nor was its intended audience easily defined in class terms. A few known artists are believed to have had 'radical' connections (C.J. Grant in particular is usually cited as a Chartist sympathiser, although any such political commitments seem to have little effect on his depiction of the urban proletariat as anything other than grotesque, ignorant and feckless.) Some scholars, notably Diana Donald, have argued that proletarian access to genteel visual culture in the late eighteenth century was widespread, and that shop windows and streets were awash with graphic images.[1] While working people undoubtedly had access to illustrated tracts, chapbooks and, increasingly, cheap periodicals in the first half of the nineteenth century, and perhaps possessed considerable skills in making sense of the iconographical and allusive qualities of wood-engraving in particular, vernacular visual culture was still largely confined to traditional genres drawn from popular narrative and devotional forms. The development of more varied and widespread modes of illustration and independent images aimed at lower-class readers between 1800 and 1850 depended largely on an opportunist ideological grasp of images as a form of dialogue, negotiation or instruction between their makers and their consumers.[2] Within this wider context, this essay forms a plea for historians, be they art historians, cultural historians or literary historians, to take more interest in one particular mode – the comic visual culture produced for the marketplace in the early Victorian period – as a major source for the study of urban society, and especially for an understanding of the lower orders and the 'shabby genteel' classes. The first half of the essay will consider some of the historiographical reasons for the relative neglect of such sources, focusing especially on issues to do with anxiety over using the *comic* mode as historical evidence. The second half will identify something of the range of under-used, little-known graphic resources available, and encourage further study of them.

It might seem that such a plea for historians to take visual culture seriously as a form of evidence no longer needs to be made. Over twenty years ago Roy Porter argued in two influential essays[3] that historians needed not just to re-evaluate their use of visual sources to 'illustrate' arguments largely, if not entirely, derived from printed sources, but also to understand the history of representation and the significance of graphic codes, and many historians have made good use of his gentle chastisement.[4] An extremely useful guide to important collections of graphic sources is available.[5] Major digitisation projects have made massive online resources easily available to the scholar – notably the digital web-based resources of the Lewis Walpole Library at Yale, the Guildhall Library in London and the John Johnson collection in the Bodleian Library, Oxford, to say nothing of more specialist resources like the Science Museum or the Wellcome Trust. There have been a few attempts to make issues to do with 'reading' graphic images an integral aspect of research self-consciousness for graduate students from whatever discipline, including my own *Reading Popular Prints*.[6] Visuality and spectacle have become central preoccupations of nineteenth-century cultural historians, producing such varied and innovative studies as John Plunkett's *Queen Victoria – First Media Monarch*, Kate Flint's *The Victorians and the Visual Imagination*, Ian Haywood's *The Revolution in Popular Literature* and Isabel Armstrong's *Victorian Glassworlds*, all of which make considerable use of visual sources.[7]

Yet a considerable history of neglect of, and indeed outright hostility towards, taking commercial *comic* image-making seriously as a historical resource still has to be overcome. Consider these comments by a major social historian writing in one of the indispensable sources for study of this kind:

> These five years [1828–1832] saw revolutionary changes in English caricature [...] the increasing use of lithography and wood engraving, the scrapbook, the illustrated newspaper [...] From about 1833 the printshops produced degenerate coloured etchings or lithographs [...] Such things have an interest for the social historian [...] they have little to do with [...] comic art.[8]

Dorothy George's belief that 'such things have an interest for the social historian' is undercut here by assumptions about the necessary relationship between 'comic art' and effective social commentary. Underlying her comments is an untroubled belief that widening the audience and democratising the codes for graphic satire in the first half of the nineteenth century inevitably compromised both the aesthetic quality and the capacity for socio-political commentary available to visual culture. George's remarks seem almost anodyne, however, when placed alongside David Kunzle's splenetic denunciation of similar material:

> The scale of [...] work suddenly shrank, corresponding to the new 1820s format for caricature, the Scrap Book – a miscellany of small vignettes, more or less loosely bound to a single theme, often casually arranged on a single

page like an artist's sketchbook and sold in a set [...] These [...] miscellanies of graphic facetiae, illustrated puns, mini-cartoons, caprices of all kind – were imitated by other artists of the period [...] The change was towards a free-wheeling comedy in which the fancy of the artist took over, but it also represented a satirical hiatus, the social impasse of a larger, less well educated audience that sought diversion rather than enlightenment, leaving the caricaturist free to say anything – or nothing in particular. This 'liberation' from the large full composition broadsheet led to a hodgepotch of inchoate miscellanies and whimsical ephemera [...] The graphic bric-a brac effect is that of a metropolitan culture spewing and sprawling itself abroad.[9]

Of course George and Kunzle were writing some time ago, and their instinctive linking of a loss of aesthetic energy within the images themselves to the needs and wants of 'a larger, less well educated audience that sought diversion rather than enlightenment' now seems a somewhat crass and simplified model of what were complex aesthetic, economic and social shifts of interest. Both writers were seeking to emphasise their own central concerns – in George's case the identification and codification of a 'great' tradition of political caricature that had evidently come to an end in the 1820s and 1830s, and in Kunzle's the establishment of the comic strip, emerging in contradistinction to caricature at this moment, as a major comic medium used powerfully across Europe and America in the nineteenth century, but little valued or exploited in Britain. Yet the effect of comments like these has been to divert attention away from comic graphic culture between 1820 and 1840 by constructing for that period a cultural black hole of comic image-making, given over to 'inchoate' populist whimsy, which existed between the decline of the political caricature and the emergence of the early Victorian black and white artists who supplied images for the novels and illustrated periodicals of the 1840s. So far, tentative attempts to recover comic image-making from this 'black hole' has been only partially successful, and it is worth considering briefly why this is so.

George and Kunzle's invocation of aesthetic criteria – 'such things have little to do with comic art' – as a means of deriding popular taste in this period has, of course, been influential in channelling art historians away from graphic satire and comedy in this period. There is no full-length study of the history of comic art in this period – the best overview remains Everitt's *English Caricaturists* which came out well over a hundred years ago.[10] Simon Houfe's extremely helpful lengthy Introduction to the 1981 edition of his *Dictionary of British Book Illustrators and Caricaturists 1800–1914* was cut from subsequent editions,[11] although of course both successive editions of Houfe's book and R.K. Engen's indispensable *Dictionary of Victorian Wood Engravers* are packed with useful information.[12] The standard dictionaries of caricature offer only limited information about the period.[13] The most persuasive attempt to re-evaluate comic art as a major source for historians has been John Marriott's six volume anthology *Unknown London* which stresses the centrality of the visual in the construction of what he calls 'early modernist' texts.[14] Not the least challenging aspect of Marriott's collection is the definition of his chosen period (1815–1845) as a coherent historical moment in the cultural formation of modernism. Apart from George Cruikshank, who has many claims to scholarly attention as an illustrator, a Dickens collaborator and a social propagandist in the temperance cause, and whose life is extensively documented and whose work remains attractive to collectors, none of the major comic artists of the period have been given detailed individual study. Robert Seymour exists largely on the strength of his Dickens connections and his 'sporting art',[15] and Thomas Hood's reputation survives, though barely flourishes, as a poet, journalist and man of letters as well as a significant comic artist and entrepreneur of visual culture.[16] Of their contemporaries, little study has been made of significant figures like William Heath, Henry Heath, Robert Cruikshank, or the young Kenny Meadows, while productive artists in downmarket comic lithography and wood-engraving like Joe Lisle, Thomas Sibson or C.J. Grant remain largely unknown.[17] Richard Pound's unpublished Ph.D. thesis on lithographed caricature magazines magnificently identifies the scholarly potential for work on comic art in the period, but considers only a very narrow range of material.[18] While images from this period appear again and again in accompaniment to scholarly studies of Victorian culture, detailed awareness of their works and their iconographical codes is seldom shown. In several instances, indeed, picture researchers and scholars have evinced a complete failure to understand the satirical intentions of images from this period. A major recent publication has offered C.J. Grant parodies of the title page of *The Penny Magazine* as significant illustrations of the 'March of Intellect' rather than as vituperative criticism of such attempts at cultural engineering.[19] Such a failure of recognition suggests a purblind approach to visual satire in the early Victorian period remains endemic.

One consequence of the sustained indifference of art history to commercial visual culture, especially graphic satire, produced in the third and fourth decades of the nineteenth century – an indifference based on a largely unexamined connection between the rise of a broader, less sophisticated consumer base for such images and a decline in their aesthetic ambition and achievement – has been a lack of interest in the collection and preservation of the mass of images produced in the period. Perhaps this neglect by libraries and other repositories is unsurprising not just because of the 'low' status accorded to it by much scholarship but also because of the nature of the material itself. Many of the early-nineteenth-century sites that exploited comic images as an integral part of their structure and appeal – songbooks, illustrated play-texts, and scraps – were designed for immediate use rather than long-term survival in libraries, and the consequence of their use within emergent locales of sociability such as the public singing room or the family parlour was their destruction. Much of the content of songbooks and play-texts was ephemeral and linked to moments of modishness or commercial fads, and thus aimed at exploiting a temporary whim of the marketplace. The diminution of scale to the pocket-sized, noted above by Kunzle as characteristic of the period and largely a recognition of the centrality of wood-engraving to the development of comic visual culture, resulted in sometimes gimcrack publishers' bindings which were both flashy yet fragile – the red quarter leather and printed paper boards of *Hood's Comic Annual*, which ran successfully for over a decade, provides a classic example of such a production. Many of the illustrated serials from the 1830s, which were central in defining the idea of the comic during this period and contained major work by artists like the Cruikshanks and Robert Seymour, were issued in paper boards.[20] Songbooks and play-texts were frequently issued in serial as well as volume form, and thus required individual binding by the consumer if they were to survive.[21] Collectors, while consistently interested in Cruikshank and the caricature tradition, have been less enthusiastic about the more downmarket, crudely drawn, small and uncoloured images which were widely offered to the market in the 1820s, 1830s, and 1840s [Fig. 1].

A Nondescript.

Fig. 1   Anonymous wood engraved illustration [Robert Cruikshank?], 'A Nondescript' in *The Comic Magazine* No. 19 (London: W. Marshall, n.d. [c. 1832?]), 111.

Nor have they been drawn to single plate lithographic caricature, perhaps put off by the interest of the genre in extreme versions of the grotesque and the vulgar [Fig. 2].

Fig. 2 Anonymous lithograph, 'The Laughing Stock No. 11' (London: O.Hodgson, n.d.).

Simply put, the mass of comic images I am interested in discussing here has survived in somewhat arbitrary and incomplete ways due to its fragility (often the result of serial issue or the use of cheap publishers' bindings) ephemerality (frequently the consequence of heavy use or the topicality of the contents) and low cultural status. Where libraries have holdings such as popular songbooks at all, they are often enshrined in rare books rooms, and frequently described as 'very rare'. Cataloguing of material in the field has consequently been non-existent or heavily delayed. The *British Museum Catalogue* concludes in 1832, with its great dynamic force, Dorothy George, as we have seen above, left contemplating an ill-defined mass of images from the 1830s that have 'nothing to do with comic art' but which 'may be of interest to the social historian'.

One further reason for the lack of scholarly awareness of comic visual culture as a resource for social historians needs to be noted. Regency and early Victorian comic art remained popular throughout the nineteenth century, and there was a considerable trade in reprinting and re-formatting images for succeeding generations of book-buyers. The continuing popularity of the

Cruikshanks, Seymour, the Heaths and their contemporaries throughout the Victorian period can be largely explained, using the kinds of models of popular culture employed by White and Stallybrass, in terms of a consistent bourgeois longing for a masculinised urban 'other' of cross-class and hence transgressive sociability that was nostalgically ascribed to Regency London. Thackeray's essays about comic art and his childhood reading perhaps express this powerful yearning most fully.[22] Yet, in order to sustain this potentially destabilising world of carnivalesque streets, grotesque human shapes and the cultural challenge of social proximity, the Victorians re-worked and re-formulated their Regency comic inheritance in a number of important ways, often by imposing firm narrative shape on a social vision that had proceeded from a primarily picaresque mode of social comprehension.

One obvious example of such a process is provided by the complex publishing history of Robert Seymour's *Sketches*. Originally released as part issue groups of images by Richard Carlile, then re-issued as five volumes of plates by Tregear, the *Sketches* by the 1840s had been drastically reduced in number and re-formulated as the occasion for two quite different accompanying texts (one by R.B. Peake and a second by Albert Forrester under his pen name of 'Crowquill') which turned the images into illustrations of a picaresque fiction, asserting in the process that Seymour's original intention had been the construction of a sporting text. While it is true that Seymour's original images did focus primarily on hunting, shooting and fishing misadventures and that he had early in his career illustrated a popular fishing book, their re-casting alongside texts for Victorian readers ensured that Seymour's subsequent primary reputation would be as a 'sporting' artist thus diverting attention away from the considerable amount of urban social satire in the original prints.[23] As a jobbing caricaturist Seymour drew on wood in the 1830s for several radical magazines, most famously *Figaro in London*,[24] as well as producing a vast number of small wood engraved comic vignettes for comic magazines, pamphlets and annuals, many of which depicted urban streets, lower-class interiors, and their often sleazy denizens, to say nothing of his great hymn to urban middling and low life, the 260 little lithographs that form *New Readings of Old Authors*[25] [Fig. 3].

Much other re-printing of Regency graphic social satire in the later Victorian period, while confirming that an interest in the urban grotesque never disappeared, similarly re-formulated Regency caricature as a proto-narrative medium in the moralistic Hogarthian model rather than accepting both its carnivalesque and its increasingly naturalistic account of urban society.[26]

There are, then, a number of reasons for the comparative neglect of the comic or satirical visual resources available for the study of the social and political experience of the lower orders in the period between 1820 and 1850

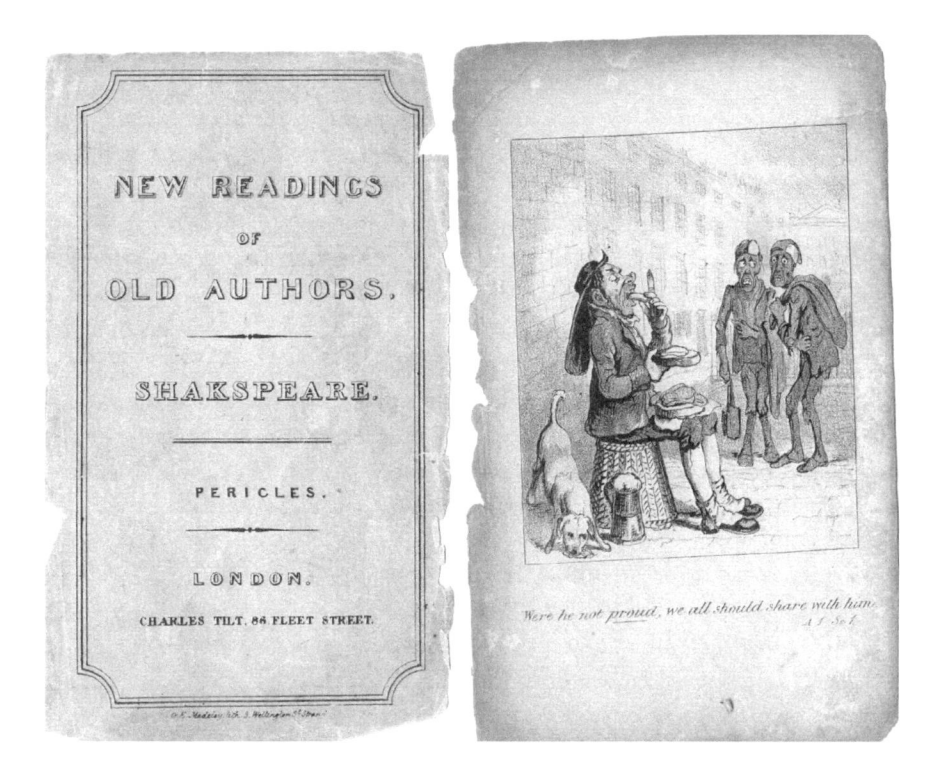

Fig. 3 Robert Seymour, Cover and lithographed image from 'Pericles' *New Readings by Old Authors* (London: Charles Tilt, n.d. [c. 1833–1834]).

– the contempt of traditional forms of art history; the relative scarcity and inaccessibility of well-focused collections and therefore of detailed catalogues and listings of available sources; the lack of a historiography which describes and assesses the history of mass-circulation modes of representation during this period; and the determination of later Victorian cultural discourses to reclaim the potentially radical vision of comic visual culture for an imagined Regency 'other' of male pleasure.

But there are two more central reasons for such neglect. The first is the recognition that visual culture at this time was, regardless of the apparent crudity of many of the prints in circulation, invariably produced, marketed and consumed within discourses that were genteel or else striving to be genteel. It follows, then, that such images are likely to tell us more about the values and fears of their producers than about the subjects represented in them. The second is the difficulty scholars have faced over the overwhelming evidence that *comedy* and *caricature* form the dominant modes through which the graphic account of the labouring classes were constructed. According to the kinds of traditional scholarly arguments represented by, most famously, White and Stallybrass,[27] urban working people provided a cultural occasion only for the rehearsal and potentially cathartic working through of rapidly formulating middle-class ideology rather than forming a representational site through which detailed understanding of the nature of the labouring-class experience might be undertaken. Fredric Jameson brilliantly summarised this view of popular culture as a form of commodification of class anxiety in *Signatures of the Visible* by arguing that mass culture is 'transformational work on social [...] anxieties and fantasies which must then have some effective presence [...] in order [...] to be "managed" or repressed'.[28] The use of comedy as the dominant representational mode and of caricature as the central aesthetic code reinforces such an apprehension of increasingly commodified visual expression during this period by inevitably evoking the well-established traditions of repulsion and contempt through which eighteenth-century caricature described the labouring poor.[29]

Put another way, scholars have found it hard to read the huge mass of comic illustration produced in the 1820s and 1830s, despite a massive shift in scale and mode as the lithograph and the vignette wood-engraving replaced single-plate etching and metal engraving at this time, as anything other than a continuation of the contemptuous dismissal of working-class culture figured in eighteenth-century caricature. In a footnote to his excellent book on American periodical illustration, Joshua Brown constructs an astute summary of the position:

> Wolff and Fox [in *The Victorian City*] note that in contrast to the *Illustrated London News*'s blinkered vision of urban society, humour magazines like *Punch* depicted poverty; but they argue that humour made sordid conditions and appearances palatable, demonstrated the innate unworthiness of the poor through their representations, and diffused any sensational impact by placing the images in a humorous (and, in the case of George Cruikshank's "Progress" tales, didactic) frame. Peter G. Buckley, in 'Comic and Social Types: From Egan to Mayhew" (paper presented at the American Historical Association Annual Meeting, New York, December 1990) suggests a different relationship, seeing the comic as a structure of feeling out of which social reportage and critique emerged.[30]

Such an intersection between recognition of the middle-class base of both the makers and consumers of visual culture and the idea of graphic comedy as a new form of naturalism, thus forming the basis of 'social critique' and 'reportage', seems to me an extremely promising place to begin serious study of graphic humour circulating in the decades immediately before Victoria's reign. And it is the shift towards the wood-engraved comic vignette, usually dropped into a text, small in scale and suggesting vigour, fluency and rapidity in its line, that forms the crucial bridge between the Regency grotesque and the new 'realism' of early Victorian reportage. The extent to which the comic wood-engraving simultaneously both enables and subverts the early Victorian drive towards realism remains a key issue for study [Fig. 4].

THE PHILOSOPHY OF LAUGHTER;
OR, MR. PUNCH IN ALL HIS GLORY.

You may sing of old Thespis, who first in a cart,
To the jolly god Bacchus enacted a part;
Miss Thalia, or Mrs. Melpomene praise,
Or to light-heeled Terpischore offer your lays;
But pray what are these, bind them all in a bunch,
Compared to the acting of Signor PUNCH?

Of Garrick, or Palmer, or Kemble, or Cooke,
Your moderns may whine, or on each write a book;
Or Matthews, or Munden, or Fawcett, suppose
They could once lead the Town as they pleas'd by the nose;
A fig for such Actors! tied all in a bunch,
Mere mortals, compared to old deified Punch!

Not Chester can charm us, nor Foote with her smile
Like the first blush of summer, our bosoms beguile,
Half so well, or so merrily drive care away,
As old Punch with his Judy in amorous play.
Kean, Young, and Macready, though thought very good,
Have heads, it is true, but then they're not of wood.
Be ye ever so dull, full of spleen or *ennui*,
Mighty Punch can enliven your spirits with glee

Fig. 4 Robert Cruikshank, Wood engraved illustration for 'The Philosophy of Laughter' in *The Spirit of the Public Journals for the Year 1825*, ed. C.M. Westmacott (London: Sherwood, Gilbert and Piper, 1826), 87.

To undertake such study would require a much more complex understanding of the wood-engraving and its social discourses than is currently available. So omnipresent was the wood-engraving in Victorian culture, and so quickly and apparently uncontroversially was it established as a medium for naturalistic reportage, that its complex and disputed origins as a medium for mass-circulation illustration in the 1820s have been largely glossed over. The medium had of course, in the cruder form of the woodcut, been long associated with the vernacular culture of the songsheet, the ballad, the chapbook and the tract. The interventionist social project of organisations like the Religious Tract Society and the Society for the Propagation of Christian Knowledge in the last decades of the eighteenth century had driven forward the potential of the wood-engraving as an expository medium for moral instruction, combining the visual codes of vernacular culture with the appeal of narrative. Genteel culture had appropriated the wood-engraving to a limited extent to form embellishments, flourishes and end-pieces to volumes of poetry. The shift of the wood-engraving into becoming the dominant visual medium of the nineteenth century, however, depended on the establishment of a wide variety of different codes for the medium: expository, aesthetic and documentary as well as comic. Yet because some of the key innovatory early Victorian experiments in print culture used the wood-engraving unselfconsciously as a 'natural' form of expression, despite it being essentially a monochrome, hastily made and linear mode, it is generally assumed that, from Bewick on, the versatility, utility and value of the medium had been accepted without question, and the only issue was how fast and how successfully the print trade could provide enough competent engravers, printers, and artists to fulfil the explosion of demand. The *Penny Magazine* (1832 onwards) normalised the wood-engraved image as an explanatory and descriptive medium, *Punch* (1841) as a comic genre, and the *Illustrated London News* (1842) as both a naturalistic medium suited to reportage and, less stridently, as medium with considerable aesthetic claims beyond the reprographic function of paintings already ascribed to it.

But in the two decades before *Punch* the comic wood-engraving had to enact a series of major shifts which both assimilated the caricature tradition and took advantage of the speed, economy and vernacular popularity that the mode made possible. In order to take advantage of the new mass readerships being formulated at this time, comic art underwent a major change in scale (essentially becoming smaller), became widely associated with a variety of circumambient text, adjusted to seriality as a major mode of distribution and consumption, and learnt to use the monochrome linearity of the wood-engraved vignette as a simultaneously expressive, decorative and humorous medium. Political and personal satire gave way, for a variety of complex reasons, to a more theatrical mode of social comedy, shifting settings from public spaces to the streets and the domestic interior. Tradespeople and their lives became an endless subject of humorous spectatorship as they struggled towards wealth and respectability – sweeps, dustmen, draymen, shopkeepers, and servants are typical subjects for comic art in the 1820s and 1830s [Fig. 5].

Fig. 5 Anonymous lithograph 'The Mud Cart Nuisance', London Nuisances No. 7 (London: W. Spooner, n.d.).

This, then, is the moment when comic art forms an extremely important witness to the social understanding of the newly visible urban labouring and small-scale trading classes. It forms a witness, in terms of content and comic mode, to the increasing interest in, and anxiety about, these classes felt by the emergent broad base of middling consumers of comic art. But, driven on by the increasing acceptance of the new medium of wood-engraving for a wide variety of representational tasks, comic art for two decades between 1820 and 1840 began to turn its caricature heritage into something closer to naturalistic reportage.

Graphic Bric-a-brac

The dialogue between contemptuous caricature representations of the labouring classes, usually formulated as expensive single-plate engraved or etched images using codes inherited from the late eighteenth century, and the emergent media of small-scale comic wood-engraving, published in a variety of new commercially experimental forms, and lithography, which was still largely using the single-plate formula, thus offers a rich and largely unexplored resource for studying working-class history [Fig. 6].

Fig. 6 George Cruikshank, Wood engraved frontispiece and title page for J. Wight, *Sunday in London* (London: Effingham Wilson, 1833).

The comic art of the two decades before the early Victorian comic preoccupation with emergent middle-class manners, pretensions and follies, evinced in the work of John Leech, Richard Doyle, Kenny Meadows, John Tenniel and their contemporaries, offers some extraordinary meetings between the comic grotesque and social realism. Some of these are well enough known sources for graphic information about urban life: George Cruikshank's work for *Mornings at Bow Street, More Mornings at Bow Street* and *Sunday in London*, all from the 1820s and 1830s, are well enough known, but such sustained publications as *The Comic Almanack* (1835–1853), described by Vogler in 1979 as epitomising 'Cruikshank's transformation of the Regency caricature into the format of Victorian book illustrations',[31] *The Universal Songster, New Readings of Old Authors, Seymour's Sketches, Hood's Annual, The Squib,* and *The Comic Offering,* [Fig. 7] all from the 1830s, let alone periodicals like *Bell's Life in London* or C.J. Grant's several serial publications, remain largely unused.

Fig. 7 Robert Seymour, Wood engraved frontispiece and title page for *The Comic Offering*, ed. Louisa Henrietta Sheridan (London: Smith, Elder, 1833).

An equally compelling project would be the tracing through of topics and formats from the emergent market-driven compulsions of commercial visual culture in the 1820s and 1830s into the early Victorian period. To give one or two obvious examples, through what mediations and developments did the picaresque comic court reports of *Mornings at Bow Street*, with its Cruikshank vignettes still in the caricature idiom, turn into 'Paul Pry's' two-volume *Oddities of London Life* (1838),[32] which combined etched full-page comic plates in a novelistic mode by Henry Heath with increasingly sociological court 'reports'; or George Hodder's *Sketches of Life and Character Taken at the Police Court* (1845) which used naturalistic full-page wood-engraved illustrations by a galaxy of contemporary comic artists including Meadows and Leech?[33] How did the rapidly drawn series of comic 'types' familiar to readers of *Bell's Life in London* turn a decade later into Kenny Meadows' ambitious *Heads of the People*, with commissioned essays from established investigative journalists accompanying a set of Meadows' images originally drawn as a sequence of Dickens extra-illustrations?[34]

Any quest for an 'authentically' working-class tradition of caricature or comic art in the Regency or early Victorian period is unlikely to be successful. Although as suggested above a number of artists have been closely associated with radical or progressive magazines in some of their work, graphic artists in this period were basically driven by the marketplace rather than any personal ideological conviction. The images available were largely 'middle brow' and thus designed for and consumed by relatively genteel and polite purchasers whose class base stretched from artisans, tradespeople and lesser white-collar workers through to the wealthy and privileged. Yet from this apparently trivial resource of comic graphic art largely designed to amuse and reassure the emergent bourgeoisie a number of major historical shifts that concern the urban poor and labouring classes can be better understood – the shift from the picaresque city to the dangerous one; the recognition of, and interest in, the domestic as well as the working lives of the urban labouring classes; the development of a fantasised 'other' of low-life licence and misbehaviour which both fascinated and appalled the newly respectable early Victorians; the cultural shifts implicit in 'the march of intellect' and the increasing literacy of the urban work force. These shifts were represented in a graphic idiom that draws heavily on the caricature tradition of the late eighteenth century, but which, in using the newly popular medium of the refined end-block wood-engraving, translated caricature into the sophisticated comic vignettes that dominated the marketplace. In moving to the wood-engraving, which was concurrently being developed as a medium for the diagrammatic display of information and for naturalistic reportage (to say nothing of its redefinition in the Bewick tradition as a self-consciously 'artistic' and aesthetic medium), comic artists were inevitably party to contemporary assumptions that the medium was an essentially *naturalistic* one. It is this new medium of what might be called 'comic naturalism' that makes comic art of the 1820s, 1830s and 1840s so suggestive a medium for the study of the street presence and the domestic life of the urban lower orders. It is only when a detailed account of emergent comic representational practices and codes in the period is made available that such resources can be fully useful to historians.

Brian Maidment

Notes

1. Diana Donald, *The Age of Caricature: Satirical Prints in the Age of George III* (New Haven, CT: Yale University Press, 1996), 1–9.
2. R.D. Altick's *The English Common Reader* (Chicago: University of Chicago Press, 1957) and Patricia Anderson's *The Printed Image and the Transformation of Popular Culture 1790–1860* (Oxford: Clarendon Press, 1991) remain the most useful introduction to such issues.
3. Roy Porter, 'Prinney, Boney, Boot', *London Review of Books* (20 March 1986), 19–20; 'Seeing the Past', *Past and Present* 118, no. 1 (February 1988), 186–205.
4. See, for an outstanding example, Vic Gattrell's *City of Laughter: Sex and Satire in Eighteenth-Century London* (London: Atlantic Books 2006).
5. Simon Turner, 'Collections of Satirical Prints in England and America', *Journal of the History of Collections* 16 no. 2 (2004), 255–65.
6. Brian Maidment, *Reading Popular Prints 1780–1870* (Manchester: Manchester University Press, 1996).
7. John Plunkett, *Queen Victoria: First Media Monarch* (Oxford: Oxford University Press, 2003); Kate Flint, *The Victorians and the Visual Imagination* (Cambridge: Cambridge University Press, 2000); Ian Haywood, *The Revolution in Popular Literature: Print, Politics and the People, 1790–1860* (Cambridge: Cambridge University Press, 2004); Isabel Armstrong, *Victorian Glassworlds* (Oxford: Oxford University Press, 2008).
8. F.G. Stephens and M.D. George, *British Museum Catalogue of Political and Personal Satires* (London: British Museum, 1874–1950, 11 vols), XI, xiii–xvii.
9. David Kunzle, *The History of the Comic Strip: The Nineteenth Century* (Berkeley: University of California Press, 1990), 20–21.
10. Graham Everitt, *English Caricaturists and Graphic Humourists of the Nineteenth Century* (London: Swan Sonnenschein & Co., 1893).
11. Simon Houfe, *The Dictionary of British Book Illustrators and Caricaturists 1800–1914* (Woodbridge: Antique Collectors' Club, revised ed. 1981) is the edition that carries Houfe's Introduction.
12. R.K. Engen, *Dictionary of Victorian Wood Engravers* (Cambridge: Chadwyck-Healey, 1985).
13. See, for example, Mark Bryant and Simon Heneage, *Dictionary of British Cartoonists and Caricaturists 1730–1980* (London: Scolar Press, 1994) or William Feaver and Ann Gould, *Masters of Caricature from Hogarth and Gillray to Scarfe and Levine* (London: Weidenfeld and Nicolson, 1981).
14. John Marriott (ed.), *Unknown London: Early Modernist Visions of the Metropolis, 1815–1845* (London: Pickering and Chatto, 2000, 6 vols).
15. Project Gutenburg has made a somewhat incoherent edition of *Seymour's Sketches* with illustrations available online.
16. Sara Lodge's sometimes polemical recent study of Hood, while outraged at a neglect which she ascribes largely to the cultural politics of the literary canon and the academy, focuses largely on the poetry. Sara Lodge, *Thomas Hood and Nineteenth Century Poetry: Work, Play and Politics* (Manchester: Manchester University Press, 2007).
17. There has been some sustained interest in Grant, largely prompted by the MA in the history of prints at University College, London. Apart from Richard Pound's Ph.D. thesis (cited below) see also R. Pound (ed.), *C.J. Grant's Political Drama: A Radical Satirist Rediscovered* (London: University College, 1998), a catalogue of an exhibition organised by students on the MA.
18. Richard Pound, 'Serial Journalism and the Transformation of English Graphic Satire 1830–1836' (unpublished Ph.D. thesis, University College London, 2002). Pound has a telling

section early in his thesis called 'Creating the canon: the obscurity of the 1830s in the history of nineteenth-century graphic satire' which describes early Victorian reactions to earlier images.
19 See, for example, John MacKenzie (ed.), *The Victorian Vision: Inventing New Britain* (London: V&A Publications, 2001), 217. The C.J. Grant illustration in MacKenzie's volume is accompanied by some detailed commentary which completely misses the satirical intention of Grant's depiction of the magazine 'diffusing knowledge of "Divinity" to the chimney sweep'.
20 See, for example, Gilbert a Beckett's *Comic Magazine* (1832–1835?), *Seymour's Comic Album* (1832?) and *The Squib Annual* (1836) which were all published in paper boards.
21 Seymour's *New Readings of Old Authors* was published in 1833 and 1834 in 26 weekly pamphlets, each in fragile paper covers with 10 lithographed images in each issue. The copy in the Yale Centre for British Art is still in the original parts as issued.
22 Thackeray was himself of course an aspiring comic artist. His essay on George Cruikshank appeared in the *Westminster Review* in June 1840, and his study of John Leech, which contains a great deal about his own youthful interest in comic illustration, in the *Quarterly Review* in December 1854.
23 As well as over 50 shooting, 10 hunting and 30 fishing images, the original *Sketches* depicted a number of sweeps, scavengers and dustmen along with many examples of street people including scavengers, beggars, coachmen, carters, drunks and urchins. Of more 'middling' trades, the *Sketches* also has bricklayers, milkmaids, soldiers, bakers, musicians, servants, pastry cooks, gardeners, and even a critic and a magazine editor.
24 Seymour's work for *The Devil in London* (March to November 1832) is less well known but equally vivid.
25 The central 'joke' of *New Readings* was the appending of subversive modern urban images to quotations largely drawn from Shakespeare, thus deflating their traditional cultural aspirations, and forming a version of the visual/verbal punning so central to Regency graphic and literary humour. *New Readings*, published probably in 1833–34 as 26 weekly instalments each containing 10 lithographs bound in paper covers, remains one of the great undiscovered texts of early nineteenth century urban investigation, combining the Regency grotesque manner with a lively-minded pleasure in urban incident and character.
26 Just to cite some obvious examples, George Cruikshank's oblong collections from the 1820s and 1830s were much reprinted. *Scraps and Sketches*, originally issued between 1828 and 1832 in four parts was re-issued in 1834 and 1854, as well as several later versions. See Albert M. Cohn *George Cruikshank: A Catalogue Raisonne* (London: The Bookman's Journal, 1924) for details. *The Comic Almanack*, which originally ran from 1835 until 1853, was reprinted many years later in volume form by John Camden Hotten and many of the original illustrations to *Bell's Life in London* were subsequently collected into volumes like Charles Hindley's *The Gallery of Comicalities* (n.d.). A detailed study of the extent to which Regency and early Victorian caricature and comic art was made available to later Victorian readers would be a useful project.
27 Allon White and Peter Stallybrass,, *The Politics and Poetics of Transgression* (London: Methuen, 1986).
28 Fredric Jameson, *Signatures of the Visible* (New York and London: Routledge, 1990), 25.
29 See, for a range of caricatures drawn from the British Museum Collection, John Brewer (ed.), *The Common People and Politics 1750–1790s* (Cambridge: Chadwyck-Healey, 1986).
30 Joshua Brown, *Beyond the Lines: Pictorial Reporting, Everyday Life, and the Crisis of Gilded Age America* (Berkeley: University of California Press, 2002), 250.

31 Vogler described *The Comic Almanack* in 1979 as deserving but lacking a scholarly commentary or edition. It still awaits its commentator and editor. See R.A. Vogler, *Graphic Works of George Cruikshank* (New York: Dover Books, 1979).
32 'Paul Pry', *Oddities of London Life* (London: Richard Bentley, 1838, 2 vols).
33 George Hodder, *Sketches of Life and Character Taken at the Police Court* (London: Sherwood and Bowyer, 1845).
34 *Heads of the People* is a book with a complex publishing history. The account of it in Martina Lauster's *Sketches of the Nineteenth Century: European Journalism and its Physiologies, 1830–1850* (Basingstoke: Palgrave Macmillan, 2007) offers a useful account of the context of the book within a tradition of urban sketches.

Language and Locale: John Locke, Somerset and Plain Style
Olivia Smith

Any biography of John Locke (1632–1704) will tell you that he was born and raised in rural Somersetshire, near Pensford, just south of Bristol. As Mark Goldie explains, 'the mainstays of the local economy were farming, woollen textiles, and, in the Mendip Hills, coal mining', and though 'Locke was to eventually die a wealthy man, his close relations included yeoman farmers and tanners'.[1] In the *Oxford Dictionary of National Biography* J.R. Milton describes Locke's family as 'very minor – indeed marginal – gentry'.[2] Alexander Popham, a local Somerset landowner and MP, nominated Locke to Westminster School, and he went up to London in his early teens to study under the famous headmaster Richard Busby. From there he proceeded to Oxford, and onward into an ever-broadening circle of *virtuosi*, politicians and aristocrats, to eventually enjoy fame in the 1690s with the publication of his *Essay Concerning Human Understanding*, the title of which proclaimed him to be a 'Gent'.[3] Locke's tombstone claims he was 'bred a scholar [who] made his learning subservient only to the cause of truth', purposefully placing him in the sphere of polite, convivial, civic-minded inquiry that Stephen Shapin and Richard Yeo have noted in the period.[4] Likewise, the 'plain' linguistic style apparently recommended by Locke's *Essay* is often traced back to literary programmes for Baconian experimental philosophy and the Royal Society, and Locke aligns himself with the gentle, communicative, scientific circle of Huygens, Boyle, Sydenham and Newton in the introduction to that book.[5] Thomas Sprat famously wrote that the members of the Royal Society had agreed to:

> reject all the amplifications, digressions, and swellings of style: to return back to the primitive purity, and shortness, when men deliver'd so many things, almost in an equal number of words. They have exacted from all their members, a close, naked, natural way of speaking; positive expressions; clear senses; a native easiness: bringing all things as near the Mathematical plainness, as they can: and preferring the language of Artizans, Countrymen, and Merchants, before that, of Wits, or Scholars.[6]

With the style of Locke's later published works in mind, this essay shows how he formulated an understanding of 'plain style' in 1659, on the eve of the Royal Society's formation, when he returned to his childhood locale of Somerset from Oxford and wrote to his university friends about the countrymen and 'artizans' he found in the west of England.[7] J.R. Milton has written that there is no evidence Locke was connected to the experimental group operating from Oxford in the 1650s that would later become the Royal Society.[8] Locke's association with Robert Boyle had begun by 1660, but he would not be elected to the Society until 1668.[9] At the turn of the 1660s Locke used similar adjectives to those Sprat would later use to describe plain style, such as 'naked', 'native' and 'natural', but these ideas were concentrated on and filtered through an appraisal of Somerset.[10] 'The cause of truth' was in Locke's mind when he went back to Somerset in 1659, and he playfully yoked it to ideas about local language, true-to-nature plainness and its antonymic artifice. This essay therefore highlights a separate seam of play centred on plain language, aside from the better-known seam of thinking associated with the Royal Society, in Locke's intellectual history.

Because of the chronological imperative of biography as a genre, Somerset is often described as an area that Locke left in order to proceed with his education, and as a consequence of this its linguistic influence on Locke is not adequately noted. Perceiving Somerset as a juvenile beginning, and writing about Locke's return to that locale as a lacuna in his development, critics often miss the point that, in visiting, thinking and writing about Somerset, Locke added to and developed his linguistic and philosophical imaginary, and expanded his idea of a plain writing style.[11] I shall therefore begin by briefly showing some of the ways in which previous writers have discussed Locke in terms of Somerset.

In the first type of linkage, Locke is depicted as a feature of Somerset. *The New Bristol Guide* of 1799 placed Locke among the natural and artificial productions of his birthplace:

> WRINGTON, ten miles S. W. from Bristol, a Market Town. Near to it is dug and prepared *Lapis Calaminaris*, which, mixed with copper, makes brais [*sic*]; it also produces *Zinc*, sometimes called Spelter) of which and copper make pinchbeck and prince's metal. Mr. *John Locke*, that excellent metaphysician, was born in this town in 1632, and died 1704. His treatises concerning human understanding, government, education, toleration, study, &c. prove him to have been one of the lights of the world, and an honor to humanity.[12]

There is poetry in this geographical mention of Locke, as he is placed in a vignette of the kind of transformative labour advocated in his *Two Treatises of Government*; we read about local productions alongside the luminous philosopher, the italics of the paragraph linking Locke typographically with Lapis Calaminaris and Zinc, raw and unformed materials in their incarnations before manufacture.[13] John Collinson's *Somerset* (1791) similarly imagined

Locke's association bringing value to Wrington, and wrote about a little thatched cottage that 'had the honour of giving birth to that celebrated philosopher'.[14] These publications are concerned with Locke's relation to Somerset simply because Locke – like a monument or battle – adds to the historical texture of that place. The way that *The New Bristol Guide* places Locke among Zinc and Lapis in their native forms chimes with ideas about natural 'roughness' that Locke played with in his Somerset letters, as we shall see below.

Secondly, it is ubiquitous to find a brief synopsis of Locke's life in the introductory pages of secondary criticism of Locke's published work and his intellectual environment, with the *Cambridge Companion to Locke* still keeping this tradition by featuring a first chapter on 'Locke's Life and Times'.[15] At the turn of the twentieth century, the Oxford professor of Logic, Thomas Fowler, described Locke as 'perhaps the greatest, but certainly the most characteristic, of English philosophers', linking this Englishness to Locke's upbringing in a Parliamentary family during the time of the civil wars, in what he called 'one of the more charming of the rural districts of England'.[16] Writing in 1908 William Osler followed Fowler in his biographical essay on Locke in *An Alabama Student*, writing of Locke's early life that he was 'the son of an attorney who at the outbreak of the civil war joined the Parliamentary side'.[17] Locke's 'Englishness', politically construed, received emphasis at this time from philosophers William Ritchie Sorley and Mary Whiton Calkins, both of whom began discussions of their subject with a description of Locke's Somerset origins, Calkins writing that '[t]he freedom of the individual is the dominant note in all the works of Locke as it is the keynote of his life'.[18] As John Marshall has recently shown, this presentation of Locke as a hereditary Parliamentarian is in no way straightforwardly accurate, but these older philosophers used Somerset as another way of encoding Locke with a loosely defined quality of 'Englishness' structured around the unique events and Parliamentary campaigns of the 1640s and 1650s, thereby linking Locke's local childhood politics to a reading of his later moral and political stance.[19] Ian Harris has presented a masterful extension to the work on Somerset, politics and Locke's later thought in his in-depth chapter on the economic, religious and social conditions of that area, explaining that things were far from the idyllic scene earlier commentators had painted and that Locke lived through the local textile depression which would have taught him that 'industry was needed for prosperity'.[20]

Thirdly and most notably Locke's Somerset childhood has been framed in book-length biographies. Adhering to the convention of their genre, the three Locke biographies that straddle the twentieth century all describe Locke's life in terms of chronological development. These biographies all therefore consider the fact that Locke was in Somerset as a child and subsequently associate the geographical area and its culture with immaturity.[21] It is crucial to projects of this nature that Locke's life moved along the clear trajectory from (to quote Maurice Cranston's first three chapter headings) 'The Somerset Child' to 'The Westminster Boy' and 'The Oxford Undergraduate'. At the end of his chapter on 'The Somerset Child', Cranston moves to the next by explaining that if Locke had not gone to Westminster school, 'he would not have had the education which was the indispensable preliminary to all that he achieved, and all that recommends his life to the biographer'.[22] Roger Woolhouse repeats this move, stating on the cusp of his move to the next chapter in his book that Locke's life 'would undoubtedly have taken a very different course had he not [...] left his home in rural Somerset' to go to school.[23] By prompting the reader to imagine alternative routes through Locke's life, these comments emphasise the fragile specificity of the historical events that created the recognisable, adult philosopher. They imbue chronologically consequent moments with great contingency, and it becomes crucial that Locke departs Somerset at the moment he did.

The chronological dynamic inherent in the structure of this type of biographical narrative is tested by the extended trip that Locke made back to Somersetshire in 1659, just over a year before his father would die. Locke was at somewhat of a caesura in his studies, having obtained his Masters from Christ Church College. From Somerset, Locke wrote back to his friends about how much he missed Oxford and the superior qualities of that place, complaining in one letter that he was 'in the midst of a company of mortall [sic] that know noething but the price of corne and sheepe', and that he wished to return to 'the injoyment of learning civility etc.' of the university town.[24] In another letter Locke wrote 'I feare I shall grow worse in a country famous for rusticks'.[25] Comments from Locke's letters depict the stay in Pensford as an unwelcome regression in his development, and seem to agree with the inconvenience of a return to his juvenile area. In one letter Locke's father advertised the prospect of Locke marrying a rich local widow.[26] Commenting on this, Cranston writes that '[n]othing came of the father's project, but the son was detained in Pensford longer than his Oxford friends thought reasonable'.[27] The charming childhood surrounds had become a place of confinement and restraint. Of the same episode Woolhouse writes that '[e]ven if the widow's money was sufficient for her and a new husband, Oxford had far more to offer'.[28] Woolhouse writes that 'The cause of the [i.e. Locke's] discontent was that rural life was no exchange for the sophistication of Oxford, the "learning [and] civility" to which he had grown accustomed.'[29] Woolhouse uses Locke's letters to show the young man's frustration, as an 'ingenious' graduate, with the simplicity of the countryside. A return to the childhood area at this stage is like driving the wrong way down the one-way street of chronological biography.

Reading against the grain of these discourses, I now show how Locke used Somerset, in 1659–60, as a sort of palette on which language experiments could be conducted.

* * *

Many of the letters that Locke wrote during this period were rhetorical and fairly ornate. Locke had a student interest in romances and literary culture; he had read French writer Jean-Louis Guez de Balzac's eloquent published letters, and could write in a courtly epistolary mode. In one early letter to William Godolphin, a friend who had also been through Westminster and Oxford, Locke describes himself as 'seeke[ing] pleasing rhetorick' at university, and J.R. Milton has explained that the young Locke 'seems to have spent a good part of his time reading lighter literature – plays, romances, and letters, much of it translated from French'.[30] Locke wrote two poems for a collection at Oxford in 1654 and another poem to celebrate the restoration of Charles II, published in 1660. Several of the letters Locke wrote back to Oxford in 1659–60 were to young women, and several unaddressed drafts have been identified by E.S. de Beer, the editor of Locke's correspondence, as probably intended for Anne Eveleigh and Elinor Parry, young women who lived at Black Hall in St. Giles, Oxford. Roger Woolhouse has explained that Locke and his friends met at Black Hall to discuss romances such as Madeleine de Scudéry's *Le Grand Cyrus* and that Locke even drafted some of his own efforts in the genre.[31] In addition to Oxonians William Uvedale and William Godolphin Locke also wrote rhetorical letters to John Strachey, another Somerset native who had gone up to Oxford.[32] As Balzac had directed some of his letters to 'Clorinda', a name from Torquato Tasso's Italian epic *La Gerusalemme liberata*, so Locke discussed French romance-writer La Calprenède's works *Cassandre* and *Cléopâtre* with one correspondent and addressed his letters variously to 'Elia, Berelisa, and Scribelia, P. E., and "Madam"'.[33] In a chapter entitled 'sentimental friendships' Cranston discussed these letters in terms of the chronological events of Locke's life, considering whether Locke was in love with any of the women addressees and how the high language indicated his true and tender emotionality.[34] Woolhouse admits that the 'emotional depth' of these letters is 'difficult to judge' and evaluates them in terms of their sincerity or insincerity, drawing a distinction between feelings that are 'real' and sentiments that are playful.[35] The 'skilful elaboration of metaphors and conceits' that Woolhouse notes Locke employing only seem to draw a smokescreen between biographer and subject. Wolfgang von Leyden wrote that the letters 'teem with expressions of affection, couched in a humorous allegorical style that is sometimes heavy and difficult to appreciate'.[36] John Yolton also took this perspective, writing of these rhetorical

Olivia Smith

letters: 'His letters are rather formal, following some of the standard models for such letters, but Locke's feelings nevertheless seem genuine'.[37] Dealing with Locke's early letters these critics take a traditionally Lockean perspective on language and imagine Locke's honest feelings flickering behind an opaque palimpsest of formulae and a calcified edifice of rhetoric. It was perhaps this presentation of Locke's letters that led J.R. Milton to surmise that they tell us 'a great deal about Locke's sentimental friendships with the ladies of Black Hall, but very little about what he was thinking, or what the intellectual issues were that had engaged his attention'.

Locke's letters do reveal that issues of the difference between transparent, truthful language and artifice preoccupied him during the summer of 1659, though it would be impossible to perceive this without engaging with the very part of the letters that Locke's biographers find distracting. Locke's views on the usefulness of anatomy for physicians as expressed in the unpublished 1668 essay 'Anatomia' provide a good explanation for why looking at these letters literally reveals only half the picture. Locke wrote that 'poreing & gazeing on the parts wch we dissect without perceiving the very precise way of their workeing is but still a superficiall knowledge'.[38] Like the body, language is a live system. The language of these letters is a game which, when followed on its own terms, yields some interesting results. Amidst more typical courtly conceits, Locke and his friends constructed their own configurations of rural areas, much of which hinged around the idea of dressing up, within which trope they discussed issues of linguistic artifice and truth in terms of the difference between the sophisticated city and the rustic country areas that several of them would return to that summer.

An early letter, tentatively dated by De Beer to the early 1650s and probably addressed to Locke's friend William Godolphin, shows the style of the conceit that would dominate Locke's letters of 1659. Locke opened with:

> Tis noe more then I expected from you that that eloquence which hath soe often left the most judicious silencd with admiration should not give me leave to speake, nor leave me the liberty of telling you handsomely how much I honour you without I borrowd the expressions from your self. [T]his I confesse I might doe but twould be a strang kinde of vanity to make ostentation of borrowd riches before the owner.[39]

This rather traditional setup, of the other lavishly adorning the character behind the writing voice with elaborate language that leaves the voice elevated beyond propriety (in this case Locke writes that Godolphin's language places him 'above the state of kings'), (mock) mute and resource-less, is extended throughout this letter with Locke writing 'Give me leave to admire your bounty which is able to bestow more then army ever fought for [...] I see you can bestow'.[40] Writing to a woman (unidentified by De Beer) in 1659 Locke used similar language to that of his earlier letter, this time exchanging imagery of flowers for imagery of riches:

> After the bestowing on me this title where in I very much pride my self I fore see I shall make but a poor returne in presenting you with the mines of a plunderd garden and when all the Flowers of both Nature and Rhetorick gatherd into one bundle would be little enough to pay my thanks, tis with shame I finde my self reducd to the necessity of sending only the refuse of others ransacking.[41]

Within the language game, Locke describes himself as unoriginal, and not worthy of such description, whereas he describes his communicants as having access to elaborate and ornate riches of language and artifice. 'You have dresd up a dull peice of clay in most choise ornaments', he writes to Anne Evelegh, adding that if he knew how 'to furnish' properly, Anne would appear in Locke's letter 'in the most curious dresse of words'; yet Locke complains that he has 'not art enough' to make this happen. In the same letter Locke writes to Anne that women can, 'with scisars and needls [...] paint and engrave and out doe the artists', and he imagines them gilding both their outsides and the reputations of their chosen friends.[42] In this letter Locke describes himself as 'a dull peice of clay', and he does the same thing in a letter to William Godolphin, describing himself as 'a shapeless lump' that Godolphin can 'fashon' into whatever form he pleases. Within the conceit, Godolphin puts Locke in a 'glorious [...] livery', he 'guild[s]' him: a process that Locke describes as being 'to clothe dull earth with flowers and gayety'.[43] Locke likens Godolphin to Deucalion, who mythically threw the bones of Gaia over his shoulder to create new people. Locke plays with Job's 'house of clay' idea – the mortal body – to create an epistolary persona for himself, as an ugly roughshod clump with 'deformitys' that can be adorned or shaped by his friends' language. He writes that Elinor Parry's pen is a 'scepter' that converts 'blots and blacknesse' into 'rays and splendor'. Locke writes: 'I could loose my self in these thoughts and look my self blinde in this dazleing radiancy'.[44]

In a letter to John Hoskins, another university friend, Locke starts joining the 'rough lump' conceit with ideas about his specific locale. He writes that although his letters are always 'clogd with imperfections', his words have become tainted by 'the clownery of the country' and 'rustick [...] importunity', and that the very air is 'churlish'.[45] Locke imagines Somersetshire altering his language and expression, and although his characterisation of the local people as types who only discourse of 'fatting of beast and dugging of ground' is, as his biographers have noted, intended insultingly, rustic language (as ventriloquised by the learned) also appears to have its benefits. As he writes to Elinor Parry at the end of a letter:

> I here in give you the greatest assureances of sincerity can be imagind since I am in a country where art hath noe share in our words and actions, you can meet with noething here but what is the innocent product of Nature and you may as well suspect daizies and daffadils to be painted as artefice in anything that comes from hence.[46]

Daisies and daffodils feature here as simple, naturally produced flowers, and are intended to have connotations of plainness and perspicuity. He continues:

> this is the only advantage I receive from this place, which I hope will be an Apologie for rudeness of this letter, aier and genius of the place carrying an antipathy to all things that are elegant and courtly which suffers me not to use ornament and rhetorick but instead thereof reality and truth.[47]

Just as elegance and courtliness are associated with ornament and rhetoric, the rustic and rural environment of Somerset is here associated with 'reality and truth'. In the same spirit, Locke wrote a very curious letter to Isaiah Ward, another friend from Oxford.[48] Though the contents of the letter to Ward show Locke defaming the country and writing of his misery at the 'animals' he is forced to converse with whilst there, after offering a derogatory description of them he signs off the letter: 'now Sir if you will admit my affection in our country dresse and downeright somerset know that I love you heartily'.[49] In this letter there are two clear permutations of 'Somerset': firstly it appears as a place with its own set of cultural frustrations, but secondly as a literary space in which sincere sentiments can be aired plainly. In the first examples above, not being able to furnish or decorate meant being less glorious than your correspondent, and less rhetorically inventive. Here not being able to furnish or decorate has the extra association with country dress, which has its own set of shortcomings that could be perceived as virtues. The 'aier and genius of the place' has an antipathy to elegance and courtliness, which on the one hand leads Locke to a description of the people as brutish, but on the other hand leads to a depiction of their language as veracious.

A letter from William Uvedale to Locke shows that, on a trip to his own parental home in Hampshire, he too thought about artifice and ornament in terms of country and city. Uvedale wrote: 'All my pleasures here are confined to a River or a Hill', which '[t]hough They are not so ravishing, are yet more innocent Then Those [i.e. those things] that are in Courtes, or citys'. Weighing up the merits of his simple river and hill against the delights of the city, Uvedale continues to say that 'there is lesse danger of a Temptation in the musick of a country voice, or conversing with the pretty Innocence of a simple girl, Then in staring upon a more beuteous and artificiall face, or frequenting onely masks, and Revells'.[50] Echoing Uvedale's earlier letter, Locke teased Elinor Parry, described above as the woman with the sceptre-like pen, that his environment comprised only 'native soile', 'a Pleaseinge walke', and 'two or 3 bonny country girles that have not one jot of dissimulation in them'.[51] For Uvedale, the whole culture of the city and court gets linked in with artifice: the painted ladies and masked balls. Locke's flirtatious letter to Elinor works on the basis of a mutual understanding of the playful merits of being able to dissimulate and conceal, deliberately describing the country girls as 'bonny', a word which connotes a specifically homely comeliness.

In December 1659 Locke experimented further with the idea of 'Somerset' language by composing a letter phonetically in a Somerset accent:

Zoft harted and vaire condicon zister
Chill tell you what cause made soe bold to write these few lines to your womanship and the rather becase chad soe vitty a messenger who could vag and zay well, nay and an honest trusty carrier chad noetheing new god wot to zend you but these tway beans the bag of the place I's doe habit I's doubt not but youl expect it most abominable kindely as though twas the hougest gay Jewell in aule the world or zomerzet shire over tis vor aule the world as cha zeen a zwinging zomerzet sheire bag puding vul of veggs and vat, disclosed in a course, but comparisons are odoriferous wherefor chill condiscend to an end.[52]

The idea of this letter is that the speaker is sending his correspondent a few local beans, which he hopes she will receive as though they were precious jewels. The style of this piece is similar to the style of the dialect poetry of actor, poet and playwright Thomas Jordan, who was one of several of Locke's contemporaries writing in this way:

Theise zitty theeves are fool'd,
That meant to do me hurt,
The Meazles could not vind my gold,
che knittne in my zhurt;

Ich che cannot chuse but zmile,
That men who can talk lattin,

> Zhould be zuch fools to take a Child
> Vor velvet, zilk, and zatten …[53]

Although dialect poetry was written to amuse gentle city dwellers who could mock the rustic dialect for its sound and pronunciation, Jordan makes the same associations as Locke in his epistle to his patron John Bence, in which he evokes the same qualities of perspicuity and honesty that Locke toyed with in the letters above:

> Sir [i.e. Bence], you will finde some pieces in this promiscuous *Gallery* very *plainly* drest, but withall very *properly*; for my aims were always rather at *aptitude* then *altitude* and to make my Compositions more genuine then gorgeous, it is no more proper in *Poets* then in Painters, to clothe a Tinker in Tissue.[54]

Jordan writes that it is inappropriate to decorate a tinker, commenting on the impropriety of ornamenting a lowly literary subject in ornate dress. Jordan mentions altitude, by which he means the way that objects can get elevated by rhetoric, and this consciousness of linguistic height was apparent in the letters of 1659, particularly in a letter that Locke wrote to John Strachey, which he filled with images of jumping and flying: 'Sir my pen is wingd for noe such flights, my thoughts trace noe such lofty steps as to lead you to those heights, and therefore must be excusd if not arrivd to that pitch'.[55] In his dialect letter about Somerset beans and bagpuddings Locke experiments with the value of gifts, asking the recipient of his letter to imbue local objects with subjective worth.

Locke repeated this manoeuvre in two letters of 1659 to Elinor Parry in which he turned his attention to gold. First he established the regular conceit of rhetoric-as-gold, writing: 'the brightnesse of the gould you send me I must confesse dazles and delights but tis the cordiall int that comforts me'.[56] Locke means it is both Elinor's form and content that animates him. In his next letter he wrote about a gift of some real coins that he was planning to (or had) sent to Elinor:

> which being stampd silver have put on a new shape to appear before you, observe what a country you have neglected to see whose very waters have not the virtue of the soe much sought philosophers stone, and let not Bath any longer be accounted amongst ordinary places whose springs are able to cure the palenesse of our bullion as well as our bodys and mak them both appear in their most lovely complexions.[57]

As De Beer points out in his notes, Locke refers to 'a way that the people of *Bath* have to give Silver Money a Golden colour' described by Joshua Childrey in his *Britannia Baconica*. Childrey describes how when silver coins are rubbed with a mixture of Bath water, mud and urine they turn temporarily gold in appearance; 'but the colour is but pale and faint, and will quickly wear off'.[58] In joining together the near-alchemical change in the silver coins and the 'curing' effect of the Bath water, Locke brings about a striking image. The function of the episode in Locke's letter is specific: here he uses the idea of the false coin (which itself represents rhetoric instead of plainness) to amuse and flatter Elinor Parry, but also as a means of emphasising the 'reality' of their friendship against the alleged artifice of traditional courtship. Locke writes of the coins:

> allow them some room in your cabinet and have some regard for silver gold as well as for silken flowers and learne of me to value these as I doe them which I esteeme the higer because they were not of the suns makeing [...] I am sure the mind wherewith they are presented ought to gaine their acceptance and you cannot be displeasd with a confidence soe suitable to a reall friendship which will not be tide always to the ceremonious rules and complement and courtship.[59]

This gesture is designed to form bonds between sender and receiver, yet it is done so self-consciously that to argue that, in the letters of this period, Locke's real sentiments are trapped in the manacles of his stale form is to attribute less skill and knowing to him and his correspondents than they appear to have had.

Locke appears to knock the 'ceremonious rules of complement and courtship', but they are the very rules that afford him such great linguistic play. Locke used the framework of affective rhetoric for further invention, commenting self-consciously on its terms and traditions while personalising them. By writing about the formal rules of courtship in the same letter as counterfeit local coins and bathing Locke purposefully exposes his rhetorical mechanism and incorporates it teasingly into his master trope of dressing and undressing. As we saw *The New Bristol Guide* serve up Somersetshire Locke alongside the raw materials of Lapis and Zinc, so Locke serves up himself and local objects for manufacture under the pens and minds of his friends. During Locke's trip to Somerset he was interested both in the warping effects of language and the idea of a 'naked' language that might convey truth.

* * *

Does the nakedness Sprat later describes in terms of the Royal Society have anything in common with the nakedness of Locke's 'rough lump' persona of 1659? The circumstantial motive for each is definitely different. Locke introduced the idea of rural roughness into a discourse of romance to entertain and flatter his friends during a period in which he might have been genuinely upset to be in Somerset; Sprat sought to publicise the scientific project. Yet Locke's Somerset letters flesh out a picture of his understanding of genre which may have informed the way he later understood the Society's 'plain' style. The two are also comparable for the way they root plainness in location. Writing in 1667 Sprat insisted that the linguistic ethos of the Royal Society was perfectly suited to the universal temper of the English, who he says 'have commonly an unaffected sincerity' and 'love to deliver their minds with a sound simplicity'. He writes that 'These Qualities are so conspicuous, and proper to our Soil [...] that even the position of our climate, the air, the influence of the heaven, the composition of the English blood; as well as the embraces of the Ocean, seem to joyn with the labours of the Royal Society, to render our Country, a Land of Experimental knowledge'.[60] Writing in 1667, Sprat claimed a national inclination to speak plainly which hinged on geographical and physical makeup, and his mentions of simplicity and unaffected sincerity chime with Locke's bonny Somerset girls and the plain (linguistic) dress worn there as opposed to worlds – perhaps like that of Locke's Oxford – that were tinted with continental romance. Sprat wrote that the English ought to be commended 'for an honourable integrity; for a neglect of circumstances, and flourishes' and 'for a scorn to deceive as well as to be deceived', and that 'Nature will reveal more of its secrets to the English, than to others'.[61]

Referring anthropomorphically to Sir Charles Cotterell's recent translation in a letter of 1659, Locke noted that *Cleopatra* was 'glad she hath learnt to speake English'.[62] Locke teased his correspondent, describing the newly translated Cleopatra as a powerful yet vanquished opponent, writing that the titular character did not have an advantage of 'beauty or any other ornament' over his correspondent's rhetorical letters. In the same year, Locke introduced the new figurative, literary, Somersetshire-based rivals of 'two or 3 bonny country girles' incapable of pretence or flourish. Going back to the questions sparked by Woolhouse, Cranston and Yolton over to what extent these letters contain real sentiment towards their female addressees, it could instead be argued that the letters capture an interesting moment in which the imagined 'bonny country girles' come in as new figures to challenge the romance heroines in the world of literary value constructed in this epistolary realm. Sprat's rubric, quoted at the start of this essay, evoked male figures in its descriptions of both plain-speakers and artificers. Locke's letters show how he was thinking along similar lines using female ciphers.

Language and Locale: John Locke, Somerset and Plain Style

Acknowledgements

I wish to thank the anonymous reader of an earlier draft of this essay for several helpful suggestions.

Notes

1. John Locke, *John Locke: Selected Correspondence*, ed. Mark Goldie (Oxford: Oxford University Press, 2002), 3.
2. J.R. Milton, 'Locke, John (1632–1704)', *Oxford Dictionary of National Biography*, Oxford University Press, Sept. 2004; online edn, May 2008, http://0-www.oxforddnb.com.catalogue.ulrls.lon.ac.uk/view/article/16885 (accessed 15 November 2009).
3. John Locke, *An Essay Concerning Human Understanding* (Oxford: The Clarendon Press, 1975), 1 (facsimile of original title page).
4. Stephen Shapin, '"A Scholar and a Gentleman": The Problematic Identity of the Scientific Practitioner in Early Modern England', *History of Science* 29, no. 3 (September 1991): 279–327; Richard Yeo, 'John Locke and Polite Philosophy' in *The Philosopher in Early Modern Europe: The Nature of a Contested Identity*, ed. Conal Condren, Stephen Gaukroger and Ian Hunter (Cambridge: Cambridge University Press, 2006), 254–75.
5. John Locke, *An Essay Concerning Human Understanding* (Oxford: The Clarendon Press, 1975), 9–10.
6. Thomas Sprat, *The History of the Royal-Society of London for the Improving of Natural Knowledge* (London, 1667), 113.
7. This article works with the dating offered by the editor of Locke's correspondence, E.S. De Beer, who worked from Locke's drafts and admitted that his dating was tentative. Locke, *The Correspondence of John Locke*, ed. E.S. De Beer (Oxford: The Clarendon Press, 1976–89), 8 vols. All letters from this edition of the *Correspondence* will be referred to below by letter number using the form Locke, *Correspondence*, L.(number).
8. Milton, 'Locke, John', *ODNB*.
9. Milton, 'Locke, John', *ODNB*.
10. For a basic summary of Sprat, Bacon and plain writing see Werner Hüllen, 'The Royal Society and the Plain Style Debate', in *Fachsprachen: Languages for Special Purposes*, ed. Hugo Steger and Herbert Ernst Wiegand (Berlin and New York: Walter de Gruyter, 1999), 2 vols, vol. 2, 2465–71.
11. An 'imaginary' in the sense of Marguerite La Caze's book *The Analytic Imaginary* (Ithaca, NY and London: Cornell University Press, 2002), 1: 'A philosophical imaginary refers to both the capacity to imagine and the stock of images philosophers use.'
12. Reverend George Heath, *The New Bristol Guide* (Bristol, 1799), 177.
13. Locke, *Two Treatises of Government*, ed. Peter Laslett (Cambridge: Cambridge University Press, 1964); see also James Tully, *A Discourse on Property: John Locke and his Adversaries* (Cambridge: Cambridge University Press, 1980), 117.
14. John Collinson, *The History and Antiquities of Somerset* (Gloucester: Alan Sutton Publishing Limited, 1983), 209.
15. *The Cambridge Companion to Locke* ed. Vere Chappell (Cambridge: Cambridge University Press, 1999).
16. Thomas Fowler, *Locke* (London: Macmillan and Co., 1880), 1–3.
17. William Osler, *An Alabama Student and Other Biographical Essays* (London: Oxford University Press, 1908), 69.

18 William Ritchie Sorley, *A History of English Philosophy* (Cambridge: Cambridge University Press, 1920); Mary Whiton Calkins, *The Persistent Problems of Philosophy* (New York: Macmillan, 1907), 492.
19 John Marshall, *John Locke: Resistance, Religion and Responsibility* (Cambridge: Cambridge University Press, 1994), 17–21; Locke, *Two Treatises of Government*, 20.
20 Ian Harris, *The Mind of John Locke: A Study of Political Theory in its Intellectual Setting* (Cambridge: Cambridge University Press, 1994), 24.
21 H.R. Fox-Bourne, *The Life of John Locke* (London: Henry S. King and Co., 1876), 2 vols; Maurice Cranston, *John Locke: A Biography* (London: Longmans, Green and Co., 1957); Roger Woolhouse, *Locke: A Biography* (Cambridge: Cambridge University Press, 2007).
22 Cranston, *John Locke: A Biography*, 17.
23 Woolhouse, *Locke: A Biography*, 10.
24 Locke, *Correspondence*, L.68.
25 Locke, *Correspondence*, L.70.
26 Locke, *Correspondence*, L.54.
27 Cranston, *John Locke: A Biography*, 55.
28 Woolhouse, *Locke: A Biography*, 23.
29 Woolhouse, *Locke: A Biography*, 23.
30 J.R. Milton, 'Locke, John'.
31 Woolhouse, *Locke: A Biography*, 24.
32 Locke, *Essays on the Law of Nature*, ed. Wolfgang von Leyden (Oxford: The Clarendon Press, 1954), 18.
33 Locke, *Correspondence*, L.62; Locke, *Essays on the Law of Nature*, 18.
34 Cranston, *John Locke: A Biography*, 47–56.
35 Woolhouse, *Locke: A Biography*, 25.
36 Von Leyden, Locke, *Essays on the Law of Nature*, 18.
37 John Yolton, *Locke: An Introduction* (Oxford: Basil Blackwell, 1985), 8.
38 Locke, 'Anatomia', included as an appendix in J.C. Walmsley, 'John Locke's Natural Philosophy (1632–1671)' (unpublished PhD thesis, Kings College London, 1998), 221–31 (225).
39 Locke, *Correspondence*, L.9.
40 Locke, *Correspondence*, L.9.
41 Locke, *Correspondence*, L.53.
42 Locke, *Correspondence*, L.65.
43 Locke, *Correspondence*, L.65; L.66.
44 Locke, *Correspondence*, L.72.
45 Locke, *Correspondence*, L.77.
46 Locke, *Correspondence*, L.80.
47 Locke, *Correspondence*, L.80.
48 Locke, *Correspondence*, vol. 1, 63n.
49 Locke, *Correspondence*, L.68.
50 Locke, *Correspondence*, L.57.
51 Locke, *Correspondence*, L.79.
52 Locke, *Correspondence*, L.88.
53 Thomas Jordan, *A Royal Arbor of Loyal Poesie* (London, 1663), 52.
54 Jordan, *A Royal Arbor of Loyal Poesie*, A2v–A3r.
55 Locke, *Correspondence*, L.50.
56 Locke, *Correspondence*, L.72.
57 Locke, *Correspondence*, L.74.

58 Locke, *Correspondence*, vol. 1, 108n; Joshua Childrey, *Britannia Baconica* (London, 1661), 33.
59 Locke, *Correspondence*, L.74.
60 Sprat, *History of the Royal Society of London*, 114.
61 Sprat, *History of the Royal Society of London*, 114–15.
62 Locke, *Correspondence*, L.62; Philip Major, '"A Credible Omen of a More Glorious Event": Sir Charles Cotterell's *Cassandra*' in *The Review of English Studies,* 60, no. 245 (2009): 406–30 gives a good account of the translation of *Cassandra*.

Institutional Culture as Whiteness: 'a complex argument'
John Higgins

Institutional culture has become a buzzword in recent discussions of higher education in South Africa.[1] Indeed, as references to it proliferate, there is a growing sense that it may well be the key to the successful 'transformation' of higher education in South Africa. Or – to frame the matter as forcefully as do many recent analysts – that it is simply the massive fact and bulk of the culture of institutions that may be the main obstacle in the way of the successful transformation of South Africa's higher education system. So it is that casual reference to it features in ministerial announcements and the mission statements of leading universities; that it is becoming increasingly the focal point of research surveys, articles, and dissertations; and that institutional culture is used to explain or explain away phenomena as different (or as related) as marking and manslaughter.[2]

In the currently dominant deployment of the term, institutional culture is used to refer to what is perceived as the overwhelming 'whiteness' of higher education in South Africa.[3] As Dean of Education at Pretoria University – and perhaps South Africa's leading controversialist in higher education matters – Jonathan Jansen put it recently, 'the last frontier in the quest for social integration and non-racial communities in former white institutions will always be this hard to define phenomenon called "institutional culture"'. In this now dominant usage, it figures as a kind of shorthand term for the powerful currents of racial feeling still active in South African society a decade after formal democratisation. Yet – as Jansen indicates – for all the apparent confidence with which the term is used, there still remains a troubling sense that it remains 'a hard to define phenomenon',[4] or, in the words of another recent commentator, a 'slippery notion indeed'.[5]

The starting-point for this essay is precisely this slipperiness, one that can perhaps best be defined as a certain tension between the term's immediate appeal, and an underlying uneasiness regarding its precise referent and related conceptual coherence. Why is it that the phrase institutional culture can come so readily to the lips yet at the same time appear so difficult to pin down, once and for all, in a singular definition?

The method of the present analysis is derived from a particular stance within contemporary literary and cultural studies, a stance I refer to elsewhere as that of a 'critical literacy'. In this sense of the term, 'critical literacy' refers to the analysis and interpretation of ideas and representations in the necessarily intricate combination of their historical, theoretical and textual dimensions. In this perspective, 'institutional culture' is treated less as an assured or given concept, one with a definite set of easily specifiable contents; it is treated rather as a 'keyword', an item of contested vocabulary in a conflictual and disputed social process. In this sense, the very fact that the phrase sounds from the lips of many educationalists may point to the difficulty of the term, as it names and by naming seeks to control a contested reality.[6] I take the idea of a 'keyword' from the work of the British literary and cultural critic, Raymond Williams (1921–1988) and a brief discussion of his use of it may help to ground the analysis that follows.[7]

Williams has been described as 'the single most important critic of postwar Britain'.[8] Williams did the most of his generation of postwar critics in Britain to emphasise the links between culture and society. Taken as a whole, his work articulated the possibility of extending the powerful analytic tools developed in the study of literature to the broader processes of cultural and political life in ways that are highly relevant to public discourse in contemporary South Africa.

Keywords: A Vocabulary of Culture and Society – first published in 1976 – represents something like a central work in Williams's *oeuvre*.[9] Subtitled a 'vocabulary of culture and society', it extends the discussion of the changing meanings of words and concepts under the pressures of social and political change. While Williams's classic study *Culture and Society 1780–1950* had focused on the shifting senses of words such as 'industry, democracy, class, art and culture', *Keywords* extended the same method of historical semantics to a much broader series of terms, ranging from 'aesthetic' and 'alienation' to 'work' and 'science'.[10] In both books – as in William's work as a whole – the guiding principle remained the same: attention to the fact that 'our vocabulary, the language we use to inquire into and to negotiate our actions, is no secondary factor, but a practical and radical element itself'.[11] As a process, the act of naming involves an agent as well as an object, and the practical lesson is that the stance or position of the agent is always involved in the (apparently neutral) description or view of the object given by the name. As we shall discover, the instability of the term 'institutional culture' arises from the fact that it looks different, depending on who is seeing it and from where, or, more accurately, who is looking for it and with what purposes in mind.

A useful starting-point for this investigation of institutional culture is Williams's entry on the word 'culture' in *Keywords*. Culture, he writes, 'is one of the two or three most complicated words in the English language',[12] and he offers a survey and summary of its various senses and definitions over the past 300 years. Much of the discussion is generally useful for any careful consideration of institutional culture, but what I want particularly to take from it is less its content than its form.[13] For the important stress in Williams's account falls on the fact of this variety, with him noting how 'it has now come to be used for important concepts in several distinct intellectual disciplines and in several distinct and incompatible systems of thought'.[14] 'Faced by [the] complex and still active use of the word', he writes, 'it is easy to react by selecting one "true" or "proper" or "scientific" sense and dismissing other senses as loose or confused'; but, he adds,

> in general it is the range and overlap of meanings that is significant. The complex of senses indicates a complex argument ... [and] within this complex argument there are fundamentally opposed as well as effectively overlapping positions ... these arguments and questions cannot be resolved by reducing the complexity of actual useage.[15]

From this densely argued perspective, what makes institutional culture so 'hard to define' is not, in the end, simply the reality it names. It is rather the fact that naming that reality is part and parcel of a series of complex arguments about the future of higher education in South Africa in which there are (in Williams's terms) 'fundamentally opposed as well as effectively overlapping positions'. Rather than seek to settle on a single 'true, proper or scientific' meaning to the term, it is then precisely the 'range and overlap of meanings' at work in the existing uses of the term that will form the focus of this investigation. In emphasising these, one aim in this essay is to contest a pervasive mode of writing in higher education discourse. For much current writing tends to deploy a vocabulary that tends to represent change (perhaps in some distantly Hegelian fashion) as an organic process, and effectively works to naturalise what I argue is better understood as a complex and disputed social action.[16]

Institutional Culture as Whiteness

A central dimension of change in South African higher education is undoubtedly the dimension of the institutional culture of university life. In one sense, South African discussion joins in a global conversation on the future of higher education; in another – and not surprisingly – it is characterised by a particularly charged and dynamic set of concerns around race that set it somewhat apart from current new public management discourse. The new public management discourse of higher education refers primarily to a sense of transformation in relation to the control and the restructuring of power relations between academics and administrators and, beyond these, on the relations between the university, society and the state. In South Africa, these concerns, while still ever present and even (as I shall argue) in fact dominant, the central focus of the discussion around the institutional culture of universities in South Africa has been on its properly *cultural* dimensions. As the ratio of black to white students at historically white universities begins to shift, and this at a different pace from that of the rate of change in the racial profile of academic staff, the cultural textures of university life itself are coming under increasing scrutiny. The new sense of institutional culture grounds – or seeks to ground it – in the perspective of those who, under the apartheid system, were denied the very possibility of a perspective: the majority of black South Africans.

From this perspective, it is argued, institutional culture is above all seen and felt as the overwhelming 'whiteness' of academic culture. 'Whiteness' here refers to the ensemble of cultural and subjective factors that together constitute the unspoken dominance of Western, European or Anglo-Saxon values and attitudes as these are reproduced and inflected in South Africa. This 'whiteness' is or can be experienced as an alienating and disempowering sense of not being fully recognised in or by the institution, and a consequent impossibility of feeling 'at home' within it. In this regard, all the well-known pressures and dilemmas of African and other post-colonial universities come into play around the now-central idea of institutional culture, and help to lend the term its considerable power and resonance in contemporary discussions.

Attempts to counter this alienation come through in a variety of ways. At the most general levels, some advocate a wholesale process of 'Africanisation' while others call for the development and implementation of policies of 'cultural justice' at the university.[17] More specifically, a number of research projects in and around the implementation of transformation at universities are now focusing on the ethnic and existential dimensions of university life.[18] For the purposes of this essay, Melissa Steyn and Mikki van Zyl's study, '"Like that Statue at Jammie Stairs …": Some student perceptions and experiences of institutional culture at the University of Cape Town in 1999', may serve as an exemplary account.[19]

First published by the Institute for Intercultural and Diversity Studies of Southern Africa in 2001, it has done much to establish the idea of 'whiteness' as the new referent for institutional culture, or at the very least, as its single most important core dimension. The study continues to serve as a reference – or even starting-point – for many new researchers in the field. In so doing, it embodies both the strengths and the weaknesses of a new usage in which the content of the term comes to refer almost exclusively to the racial dimensions or aspects of university life, with some emphasis on how these impact on pedagogic communication.

The core definitions refer to, or confidently assume, the general understanding of institutional culture as 'the prevailing ethos – the deep-seated set of norms, assumptions and values that predominate and pervade most of the environment'.[20] Institutional culture is the

> 'sum total' effects of the values, attitudes, styles of interaction, collective memories – the 'way of life' of the university, known by those who work and study in the university environment, through their lived experience.[21]

As 'sum total', the term has the capacity to refer to any and every aspect of experience at university, from parking to policing, from the sites and names of buildings to any and every joke told on campus.[22]

At the centre of Steyn and van Zyl's study is the assertion that 'whiteness' stands as the unacknowledged core of the University of Cape Town's institutional culture.[23] In the Abstract that heads the document, the claim is that 'it is clear that in students' experiences "whiteness" still largely characterizes the institutional culture'. In line with this, they argue that it 'has been shaped by a very specific historical cultural positioning, and the world view which informs this position has been normalised within the UCT environment. To a large extent this cultural milieu has been characterized by "whiteness"'.[24] And, summarising their sample of student opinion, they conclude that 'the assumption is that the white norm fits all'.[25] Not surprisingly, the final conclusions and recommendations suggest that 'Student testimonies reflect that the university unquestionably subscribes to the ideology of whiteness'. All in all, the 'perceived lack of attention paid to institutional culture ... is experienced both as a symptom and consequence of this culture of whiteness'.[26]

'Whiteness' is a key term taken from discussions around multiculturalism, largely in the USA. Several references are made in the survey to essays in David Theo Goldberg's seminal anthology, *Multiculturalism: A Critical Reader* and particular use is made of Peter McLaren's article, 'White Terror and Oppositional Agency: Towards a Critical Multiculturalism'.[27] Steyn and van Zyl take from McLaren the centrality he gives to the notion of 'whiteness' as a central unacknowledged category in Western society and education.

For McLaren, 'white culture's most formidable attribute is its ability to mask itself as a category'.[28] '[U]nless we give white students a sense of their own identity as an emergent ethnicity' he argues, 'we naturalize whiteness as a cultural marker against which Otherness is defined'. 'White groups', he writes

> need to examine their own ethnic histories so that they are less likely to judge their own cultural norms as neutral and universal ... Whiteness does not exist outside of culture but constitutes the prevailing social text in which social norms are made and remade.

Whiteness, he concludes, 'has become the invisible norm for how the dominant culture measures its own worth and civility'.[29]

Many of the details of Steyn and van Zyl's account work to echo and confirm McLaren's argument. Some students reported feelings of alienation and anomie, and maintained that 'UCT is Eurocentric in tradition and practice'.[30] Others believed that 'the institutional culture would only really change if the white section of the university made a conscious effort to open up to learning, rather than assuming that "others" were the only ones in deficit'.[31]

The central and repeated point – of 'whiteness' as the 'invisible norm' – offers a powerful new perspective on the institutional cultures of South African universities. The varied testimonies point to the difficulties and possibilities of dealing with this aspect of socially pervasive though often subliminal racism 'still at work' ten years after the formal demise of apartheid.[32] The findings call for an intensive consciousness-raising around the issue of whiteness similar in scope to the great consciousness-raising around patriarchalism enjoined by feminism in the 1960s and 1970s: a 'conscious deliberate attempt to examine and question the "normal"'.[33] This would include, in the first instance, a commitment to education and training around 'whiteness' in pedagogical and other sites of intersubjective exchange on campus. These and other recommendations from the survey continue to serve as useful guidelines for further initiatives, both at UCT and elsewhere.[34]

At the same time, a number of visible inconsistencies and theoretical difficulties emerge within and from the report's deployment of institutional culture as whiteness. These have to do with the explanatory centrality apparently assigned to whiteness in its survey and summary of student experience and perception.

The general theoretical problem may well be that of the tension between contrasting 'objectivist' and 'subjectivist' strands in sociological analysis, and it comes through in this survey as a problem of translation.[35] For while the study as a whole claims that nothing can be achieved 'without understanding the sense-making of the students themselves',[36] they acknowledge that students 'may not always be able to articulate exactly what it is that they experience'.[37] The survey, for instance, claims that most of the students 'who discussed the issue of UCT's institutional culture, had a solid grasp of its relation to institutional power – they could identify the centre, and the resultant tension of those on the margins';[38] but it remains unclear whether the key terms of centre, margins, institutional power and institutional culture itself are the terms actually used by the students themselves, or the translated terms of the interviewers ascribed to the students. The danger throughout is one of a certain circularity, in which the central explanatory category of 'whiteness' is at one point taken as the starting-point of the analysis, but at another is represented as an end result or as a conclusion derived from it. The formulations vary, and seem to embody the always difficult interpretive transaction that takes place between interviewer and interviewee.[39]

For a classic 'objectivist' sociologist such as Durkheim, 'social life must be explained not by the conception of those who participate in it, but by the deep causes which lie outside of consciousness'.[40] No mere survey of opinion, based on personal experiences, would have a chance of getting through to the underlying causes of alienation and anomie in an institutional culture like that of the university. Yet, at the same time, the richness of texture enabled by subjective accounts is a resource no sociologist can ignore, and particularly one who wishes to locate the dynamics of agency within structural constraint, and to resist the tendency to reduce the respondent in the interview to an object of analysis.[41] The middle-ground is hard – if not impossible – to find; but a stricter attention to the inevitable complications of the process than is evident in the survey might have yielded less problematic results.[42]

It is for these and other related reasons that many sociologists suggest a control on opinion surveys – including those done by in-depth interview – through two related procedures. The first is in terms of internal coherence, necessitating a very careful scrutiny of the match between data and explanation; the second, an external check through the comparative application of other explanatory hypotheses, existing elsewhere in the literature.[43]

In terms of the survey's internal coherence, two problems emerge. First of all, a certain undermining of the explanatory primacy of whiteness emerges from the report's own attention to significant cultural divisions within the black student body itself, a body assigned an essential unity in the binary oppositions engaged by whiteness critique. Significant divisions are reported between black students from Model C schools and those from poorer schools (often paralleling or reinforcing a divide between those from urban and rural backgrounds). The significant division here between different schooling at primary and secondary levels undermines the cohesiveness of a purely racial categorisation such as whiteness as the primary explanatory factor in experiences of alienation within higher education; and it may well be that such alienation is perhaps better viewed as part and parcel of a structure of racialised rather than racial inequalities.[44]

Secondly, there is the uneasy way in which whiteness is joined as a vantage-point for critique by questions raised by issues of sexual orientation, gender, and disability. In the report, these come together as simply different aspects of the general power relations at work in the institutional culture of the university; but this again undermines the report's general claim (illustrated above) for the central explanatory role apparently given to whiteness. This is particularly apparent in those moments where a vocabulary of centredness replaces or subsumes that of whiteness, as, for instance, in the Executive Summary which precedes the report proper. This paraphrases the arguments that follow as indicating 'that those who were in subject positionalities that are centred were able to move through the university a great deal more comfortably than those toward the margins' and goes on to explain that 'these centres include: whiteness, Euro-American worldview, English-speaking as mother-tongue, maleness, heterosexuality, able-bodiedness, (upper) middle-class-ness, South African nationality, urban background, etc.'.[45]

In theoretical terms, these inconsistencies suggests that whiteness alone does not play the primary role in institutional culture that the report appears generally to ascribe to it. Whiteness may instead be better regarded as just one (and secondary or over-determined) factor amongst others, such as the maleness, heterosexuality, able-bodiedness, urban background and/or South African nationality mentioned in the survey. The existence of such internal inconsistencies suggests a strong need for the consideration of alternative explanations, and prime amongst them, perhaps, Pierre Bourdieu's notable theories of education and social reproduction. For Bourdieu's writings are particularly attuned to the feelings of alienation and anomie at work in education systems. Indeed, the existence of such feelings are held to play a constitutive rather than (as it were) incidental role in social reproduction as a whole.[46]

Many of the feelings expressed by students in the Steyn and van Zyl report correspond very strongly to the dilemma faced by the working-classes and lower-middle-classes in a higher education system geared to the success of the already privileged. For these – in Bourdieu's terms, the 'naturally' distinguished – the institutional culture of higher education poses no problems of adaption. They 'merely need to be what they are in order to be what they have to be, that is, naturally distinguished from those who are obliged to struggle for distinction'.[47] In this struggle for distinction (the cultural marker of social and economic privilege), the natural is, of course, the precisely constituted materiality of prior privilege that makes even the most democratic educational structures still a prey to social and economic inequalities. All in all, Steyn and van Zyl's account, in placing its main emphasis on 'whiteness' as racial differentiation, tends to *background* (if we may reverse the more usual term 'to foreground') the broader issues of reproduction and cultural capital at the heart of Bourdieu's account.[48]

If, indeed, Bourdieu's insights can help to smooth out several contradictory findings in Steyn and van Zyl's survey, this works to suggest that though race may be an obvious and immediate factor in the experience of alienation and anomie, it may well be a secondary phenomenon in terms of explanation. Race is secondary in other words to the deeper logic of social subordination and reproduction that divides racial groups internally according to the force of class distinction.[49] This, indeed, is the general conclusion of many of the contributors in Goldberg's anthology (and elsewhere) who argue that multiculturalism needs to be attuned to the material conditions of cultural differentiation.[50]

Certainly, one of the surely unintended consequences of a focus on institutional culture as whiteness is a consequent marginalisation of the changes occurring at the interface between academics and administrators (and beyond these, universities and the state). This interface also forms an important aspect, dimension or referent for debates around institutional culture, though one somewhat overshadowed by the currently dominant definition discussed above.

Whose Institutional Culture? Academics versus Administrators

Although the sense of institutional culture as whiteness is dominant in South African discussions, a second sense is also present and in use, though overshadowed by the first. This second sense connects more directly to overseas debates, and addresses a powerful trend in university systems across the world, as well as in one dimension of what transformation in South African higher education has meant in practice. It understands and defines the idea from the standpoint of the newly emerging interests that are usually referred to as the 'new managerialism'.[51]

From this standpoint, in Bill Readings's succinct characterization, 'the administrator rather than the professor [becomes] the central figure of the University' while the university as a whole is subjected to a 'generalized logic of "accountability" in which the University must pursue "excellence" in all aspects of its functioning'.[52] In this use, institutional culture refers to the site of a conflict and contest between two different and opposing definitions of the purpose of higher education, definitions that are uneasily conjoined in South African policy.

The first of these – akin to the values of academic freedom embodied in the 'English liberal' view of the university's social function – comes through in the repeated emphasis, in South African policy, on the development of 'critical citizenship', and the need for an educated citizenship for the promotion and development of democracy. A central aim of higher education from this perspective is thus described as 'the socialization of enlightened, responsive and constructively critical citizens'.[53] This point of view sees higher education as playing a constitutive role in the development of a democratic society, in a line of thought extending at least as far back as Immanuel Kant's championing of Enlightenment values, and particularly the value of public deliberation, in his seminal essay 'An Answer to the Question: "What is Enlightenment?"'.[54]

The second is more in line with the state-centred view of higher education promoted by the Afrikaans establishment, but now carried forward in the post-apartheid state, and in line with neo-liberal policies across the globe. It emphasises the need to 'address the development needs of society and provide the labour market, in a knowledge-driven and knowledge-dependent society, with the ever-changing high-level competencies and expertise necessary for the growth and prosperity of a modern economy'.[55] From this perspective, education and higher education needs to be carefully controlled and directed, and 'taylored' (if you'll excuse the pun) to the dynamics of the economy. It sees education and higher education as playing a largely instrumental role, and one subordinated to the state's interpretation of economic needs.

The *mot d'ordre* from one of the champions of the idea of institutional culture in business studies – Edgar Schein – appears, in fact, to have resonated strongly with South African administrators. 'Organizational cultures', he wrote in his seminal study of 1975, 'are created by leaders, and one of the most decisive functions of leadership may be the creation, the management, and – if and when that may become necessary – the destruction of a culture'.[56] In an interesting attempt to turn the tables, institutional culture became the name for academic culture itself, as the substance of what was being attacked and threatened by the new managerialism.

In a useful survey of post-apartheid South African higher education policy, Gibbon and Kabaki suggest that 'by 1998, the emphasis [in government policy] had decisively shifted from demands for democratisation to demands for efficiency and effectiveness' with a consequently important shift in the balance of power between academics and administrators. Research showed that 'the overwhelming majority of [academic] respondents felt that their relationship with management had been reconfigured in a way that now defined them as subordinate employees rather than colleagues'.[57] One of the prime effects of 'transformation' was a definite shift from 'academic self-rule to academic managerialism',[58] with an increasing salary gap developing between senior managers and senior academics (from a ratio of 2:1 during the late 1980s to a ration of 4.5:1 in the late 1990s).[59] In this assessment, the '"democratic phase" currently being experienced by South African institutions had long since been superceded in the developed nations by the "managerial phase"'.[60] That this phase represents an attack on rather than a dialogue with and improvement of academic culture – an intuition present implicitly in many responses to the pressures of neo-liberal change – was explicitly stated and argued by Olajide Oloyede.[61]

John Higgins

Writing in response to managerial changes at the University of Fort Hare, Oloyede argues that it is precisely that 'destruction of a culture' (championed by Schein) that academic culture is threatened with in South Africa. He sums up his case in the following terms: 'My main goal is to alert those involved in the transformation of universities to the fact that universities are fragmented into diverse disciplinary cultures and as such are loose and complex organizations. Precisely because of this, management discourse is not sufficient and cannot be the basis for the effective and efficient steering of the university'.[62] '"False managerialism" tries to force disciplines into the same mould, impose crude accountability and over-simplified indicators of performance which are hardly appropriate to academic work.' Yet, asserts Oloyede,

> disciplinary values and cultures are critical for any effective steering of the university. This is because in each discipline, there exists a 'self-organized' collective control which tends to take quite different forms from that of official regulation. This is grounded in collegiality ... To this extent, roles, norms, values, beliefs and ideology – generally referred to as *organizational culture* – serve as the essential elements of interaction.[63]

In this deployment, we see something of a repetition of the dynamics of the term present in the earlier uses in business writing.[64] Institutional culture is what has to be controlled or managed by the colonising administrator; it is what has to be defended by the academic worker. The dispute over programmes – perhaps the first concrete point of higher education policy in South Africa that placed administrators and academics in more or less direct conflict – similarly reveals the constitutive contradiction at work within institutional culture, and the contradictory roles it plays.[65] As an instrumental concept, it appears to promise successful control over institutions for managers, while for academics resisting imposed change, it refers to the substance of their practical activity as teachers and researchers.

Conclusion

As Williams reminded us, and as this brief discussion of different uses of the term has shown, the act of naming involves an agent as well as an object. The instability of the term institutional culture – its capacity to name different things, or to refer to different aspects of the same complex object – arises from the fact that institutional culture looks different, depending on who is seeing it and from where; or, more accurately, who is looking for it and with what purposes in mind. Though a singular name, its referent is best understood as multiple and complex, in ways that most users of it tend to ignore in the passion of their arguments.

If much of the overseas discussion of institutional culture focused on the institutional aspects, we have seen how in South Africa the main focus of interest shifted to its cultural aspects and dimensions. Many discussions here in South Africa have, above all, emphasised the need for a thoroughgoing critique of the dominant whiteness of institutional culture in higher education. However, as we saw above, while the focus of this critique brought some strong feelings to light, these discussions were weakened by a tendency to over-unify the category of race. Even the most powerful of these analyses would, in any event have to take into account Henry Louis Gates's astute point that 'a redistributionist agenda may not even be intelligible with respect to cultural capital [since] once cultural knowledge is redistributed so that it fails to mark a distinction, it loses its value [...].' Following Bourdieu, Gates's hard lesson is that while the currency of cultural capital (and by extension, institutional culture) can change, it is likely to leave intact the structures of distinction that support it. The question 'What could confer "equity" on "culture"?' is, he argues, unanswerable within a divided and unequal society.[66]

In more general terms, it may also be that too exclusive an emphasis on whiteness also runs the risk – common to many postcolonial societies – of reaffirming the very racial categories and identities that the new postcolonial orders sought to disperse. In her powerful survey, 'Race and Identity in the Nation', Zimitri Erasmus warns of the dangers of equity policies that in fact 'perpetuate apartheid race categories and race thinking'.[67] At one and the same time, she recommends, it is important 'to remember and recognise the historical legacies of race and white supremacy and their influence on the present' while also moving away from 'holding onto race as a form of cultural and political armour'.[68] 'The challenge before us', she concludes, 'is to find ways of recognising race and its continued effects on people's every day lives, in an attempt to work against racial inequality, while at the same time working against practices that perpetuate race thinking'.[69] Acceptance of this challenge is the difficult task that faces those participating in the ongoing debates around institutional culture.

It may be that in the end institutional culture is less of a concept than a representation. As such, it screens a number of problems, in both opposed senses of the term. It serves as a surface on which various social contradictions and tensions can be projected, while at the same time, often disguising or translating these into other terms according to the dynamics of displacement.[70] It is a term that mimes conceptual density, but lacks conceptual force, while its apparently appealing explanatory force is often undermined by its actual contents. All in all – as this essay has tried to indicate – it is a term that requires the careful unpacking and analysis associated with the real strengths of Williams's cultural materialist project as it reminds us of the difficulties associated with every 'complex argument'.[71]

Notes

1. The following essay owes much to research originally commissioned by the Council on Higher Education in South Africa. For this, see John Higgins, 'Institutional Culture as Keyword', in *Review of Higher Education in South Africa: Selected Themes* (Pretoria: Council on Higher Education, 2007), 97–122.
2. See, for instance, Kader Asmal's comment on President Mbeki's meeting with Higher Education Working Group in Pretoria, Thursday 11th December 2003: 'Among other challenges that lay ahead, said Prof. Asmal, were transformation, curriculum development, and cultural justice. The latter entails building a more inclusive institutional culture that embraced language and cultural diversity among staff and students', South Africa Means Business, 'Mbeki meets higher education Group', news@sameansbiz.co.za (accessed 26 March 2006); Zimitri Erasmus and Jacques de Wet, 'Not Naming "Race": Some Medical Students' Experiences and Perceptions of "Race" and Racism in the Health Sciences Faculty of the University of Cape Town' (Research report for the Institute for Intercultural and Diversity Studies at UCT, 2003); Salma Ismail, 'An Investigation into Staff Members' Experiences of Institutional Culture at the University of Cape Town' (Research report for the Institutional Culture Working Group of the Employment Equity Forum at UCT, 2000); Salma Ismail, 'Diversity Intervention for Health Educators: A Detailed Description of Diversity Workshops with Health Educators at UCT' (Research report for the Institute for Intercultural and Diversity Studies at UCT, 2002); Njabulo Ndebele, 'The way forward for the University of Cape Town' (Preface to Organizational Climate Survey, UCT, 2004); Damian Ruth 'The Stories We Tell and the Way We Tell Them: An investigation into the institutional culture of the University of the North, South Africa' (Research report for AAU. (n.d.)); Melissa Steyn and Mikki van Zyl, '"Like that Statue at Jammie Stairs …": Some student perceptions and experiences of institutional culture at the University of Cape Town in 1999' (Research report for the Institute for Intercultural and Diversity Studies at UCT, 2001); Cecilia M. du Toit, 'Transforming and managing the organizational culture of a university to meet the challenges of a changing environment', *South African Journal of Higher Education* 10, no. 1 (1996): 96–104. The use of closed marking books at UCT, and much of the internal public commentary on the Hahn murder case at UCT, where a professor was attacked and killed by a former Ph.D. student, also deploy the term.
3. 'Whiteness' is a term developed in critical multicultural writing in the USA to designate the blindness of white culture to its own assumptions, and its relative blindness to the other. In South Africa, the term has notably been picked up by Melissa Steyn, and forms the basis of her study of institutional culture at UCT (Steyn and van Zyl, 'Like that Statue at Jammie Stairs').
4. Jonathan Jansen, 'How Far Have We Come?', *Mail and Guardian*, 13th–19th August 2004, Getting Ahead Supplement, 1.
5. Paula Ensor, 'Curriculum', in *Transformation in Higher Education*, ed. Nico Cloete et al. (Lansdowne: Centre for Higher Education Transformation, 2002), 285.
6. See John Higgins, '"It's Literacy, Stupid!" – Declining the Humanities in NRF Research Policy' *Journal of Higher Education in Africa* 5, no. 1 (2007): 95–112; John Higgins, 'Critical Literacies: English Studies Beyond the Canon', *Journal of Literary Studies* 8,

nos 3–4 (1992): 86-100; and note 7 below. Interestingly, a similarly sceptical stance underlies much of Adorno's work. See, for instance, his distrust of what he refers to as the 'harmonistic tendency' in much sociological analysis, what he describes as the 'tendency to explain away the constitutive contradictions on which our society rests, to conjure them out of existence'. See Theodor Adorno, *Introduction to Sociology* (Stanford, CA: Stanford University Press, 2000), 7.

7 For much of this, see John Higgins, *Raymond Williams: Literature, Marxism and Cultural Materialism* (London and New York: Routledge, 1999), and, with especial reference to Williams's *Keywords*, 'Raymond Williams, Keywords and Deconstruction', *Key Words* 4 (2006), 40–55. Compare also Christopher Norris's astute comments in his '*Keywords*, Ideology and Critical Theory' in *Raymond Williams Now*, ed. Jeff Wallace, Rod Jones and Sophie Nield (New York: St Martin's Press, 1997).

8 Terry Eagleton, *The Function of Criticism: From The Spectator to Post-Structuralism* (London: Verso, 1984), 108.

9 Raymond Williams, *Keywords: A Vocabulary of Culture and Society* (London: Fontana, 1983, 2nd edn). References here are taken from the second, revised and expanded edition of 1983.

10 Raymond Williams, *Culture and Society 1780–1950* (Harmondsworth: Penguin, 1979), 13.

11 Williams, *Culture and Society*, 323.

12 Williams, *Keywords*, 87.

13 In particular, his attention to the metaphorical shift in the use of the term, from its original meaning as the tending and cultivation of crops, to the 'process of human development', and used with reference to various forms of education, is particularly valuable. Also useful is the attention to Herder's criticism of Euro-centrism in his *Ideas on the Philosophy of the History of Mankind* (1784–1791), where he asserts that the 'very thought of a superior European culture is a blatant insult to the majesty of Nature' (cited Williams, *Keywords*, 89). For a useful selection and presentation of key texts representing Enlightenment views of race, including a relevant portion of Herder's study and Immanuel Kant's critical response to it, see Emmanuel Chukwudi Eze (ed.), *Race and the Enlightenment: A Reader* (Oxford: Blackwell, 1997), especially 65–78.

14 Williams, *Keywords*, 87.

15 Williams, *Keywords*, 91.

16 Much the same point forms a part of my critique of Bill Readings' useful and provocative study, *The University in Ruins* (Cambridge, MA and London: Harvard University Press, 1996): see John Higgins, 'Academic Freedom and the University', *Cultural Values* 4, no. 3 (2000): 352–73; and also of some recent work by André du Toit: see John Higgins, 'From Academic Analysis to Apparatchik Thinking: A Reply to André du Toit', in *Pretexts: Literary and Cultural Studies* 12, no. 2 (2003): 191–97.

17 See, for instance, Chirevo V. Kwenda's useful article, 'Cultural Justice: The pathway to reconciliation and social cohesion', in *What Holds Us Together: Social Cohesion in South Africa*, ed. David Chidester, Phillip Dexter and Wilmot James (Cape Town: HSRC Press, 2003). More generally, see also J.F. Ade Ajayi, Lameck, K.H. Goma, and G. Ampah Johnson, *The African Experience with Higher Education* (London: James Currey, 1996).

18 See, for instance, the work of the University of Western Cape research group on institutional culture, and notably, Lionel Thaver's work within that group. Lionel Thaver, '"At Home" – Institutional Culture and Higher Education: Some methodological considerations'. Unpublished paper prepared for the Institutional Culture Research Group, 2004.

19 Steyn and van Zyl, '"Like that Statue at Jammie Stairs"'.

20 Steyn and van Zyl, '"Like that Statue at Jammie Stairs"', x.

21 Steyn and van Zyl, "'Like that Statue at Jammie Stairs'", 20
22 Steyn and van Zyl, "'Like that Statue at Jammie Stairs'", 27, 28, 42.
23 And, by extension, and for all their differences, that of the other historically white universities in South Africa.
24 Steyn and van Zyl, "'Like that Statue at Jammie Stairs'", iii.
25 Steyn and van Zyl, "'Like that Statue at Jammie Stairs'", 37.
26 Steyn and van Zyl, "'Like that Statue at Jammie Stairs'", 68.
27 See David Theo Goldberg (ed.), *Multiculturalism: A Critical Reader* (Oxford: Basil Blackwell, 1995) and particularly Peter McLaren's chapter, 'White Terror and Oppositional Agency: Towards a Critical Multiculturalism'. Frantz Fanon's discussion in *Black Skin, White Masks* may be regarded as the starting-point for critiques of 'whiteness'. Frantz Fanon, *Black Skin, White Masks*, trans. C.L. Markmann (New York: Grove Press, 1967). As he wrote there, 'His metaphysics, or, less pretentiously, his customs and the sources on which they were based, were wiped out because they were in conflict with a civilization that he did not know and that was imposed on him … The white world, the only honourable one, barred me from all participation' (pp. 110, 114). For some contemporary discussion, see also bell hooks, *Black Looks: Race and Representation* (Boston: South End Press, 1992) and Cornel West, *Race Matters* (Boston: Beacon Press, 1993). For further discussions, see, for instance, Cornel West, 'The New Cultural Politics of Difference', in *Out There: Marginalization and Contemporary Cultures*, ed. R. Ferguson, M. Gever, T.T. Minh-Ha and Cornel West (Cambridge: MIT, 1990).
28 McLaren, 'White Terror and Oppositional Agency', 61.
29 McLaren, 'White Terror and Oppositional Agency', 59. The stance is common to most of the contributors in Goldberg's collection. For the pedagogical implications, see especially Henry Giroux, 'Insurgent Multiculturalism and the Promise of Pedagogy', in Goldberg (ed.), *Multiculturalism*.
30 Steyn and van Zyl, "'Like that Statue at Jammie Stairs'", 69.
31 Steyn and van Zyl, "'Like that Statue at Jammie Stairs'", 66.
32 For a powerful and probing account of the concept of 'subliminal racism', see Ulrike Kistner, 'The Elided Performative', in *Commissioning and Contesting Post-Apartheid's Human Rights* (Munster: Lit. Verlag, 2003).
33 Steyn and van Zyl, "'Like that Statue at Jammie Stairs'", 29.
34 At UCT, see especially the continuing work of the Institute for Intercultural and Diversity Studies of Southern Africa, and particularly the ongoing work in the Health Sciences Faculty: Ismail, 'An Investigation into Staff Members' Experiences of Institutional Culture at the University of Cape Town'; and Erasmus and de Wet, 'Not Naming "Race"'.
35 I leave aside the more problematic dimension of the translation of experience itself in terms of the Freudian concept of transference. This attends to the ways in which the subject's most apparently spontaneous experiences in the present are in reality strongly influenced by past traumas. As opposed to this repetition, psychoanalysis seeks a working through that allows the analysand to 're-experience some portion of his [sic] forgotten life, but must see to it, on the other hand, that the [analysand] retains some degree of aloofness, which will enable him, in spite of everything, to recognise that what appears to be reality is in fact only a repetition of a forgotten past'. Sigmund Freud, *Standard Edition of the Complete Psychological Works of Sigmund Freud*, trans. J. Strachey, 24 vols (London: Hogarth Press, 1943–1974). Given the psychodynamics of the teaching situation, transference plays a significant role in much student–teacher interaction in both positive (it is, after all, the source of the learning impulse itself) as well as negative ways.
36 Steyn and van Zyl, "'Like that Statue at Jammie Stairs'", 2.
37 Steyn and van Zyl, "'Like that Statue at Jammie Stairs'", n.p.

38 Steyn and van Zyl, '"Like that Statue at Jammie Stairs"', 36.
39 The lack is somewhat surprising given the attention paid precisely to this problem in McLaren's account, one of the acknowledged sources of the survey.
40 Cited in Pierre Bourdieu, *In Other Words*, trans. R. Nice (Oxford: Polity Press, 1990), 125.
41 For useful general discussions of these tensions, see, for instance, Anthony Giddens, *Central Problems in Social Theory: Action, Structure and Contradiction in Social Analysis.* (London: Macmillan, 1979), and particularly chapter 2, 'Agency, Structure'; and Pierre Bourdieu, *The Logic of Practice*, trans. R. Nice (Oxford: Polity Press, 1990).
42 Bourdieu's analysis of the dynamics of the interview situation is particularly useful here. See especially his insistence that 'Social agents do not innately possess a science of what they are and what they do. More precisely, they do not necessarily have access to the core principles of their discontent or their malaise, and, without aiming to mislead, their most spontaneous declarations may express something quite different from what they seem to say.' Pierre Bourdieu et al., *The Weight of the World: Social Suffering in Contemporary* Society, trans. P.P. Ferguson (Stanford: Stanford University Press, 1999) 620. The essay's warnings regarding style and point of view could usefully supplement the current discussion of the Steyn and van Zyl report, '"Like that Statue at Jammie Stairs"'.
43 Giddens, for instance, in his standard account of sociological practice, recommends some form of triangulation to seek to lessen the problems arising from situations in which the influence of the interviewer may be present. See Anthony Giddens, *Sociology* (Oxford: Polity, 1989), 679–83.
44 A finding significantly echoed in much other research. Compare, for instance, Erasmus's comment: on how an 'essentialist way of working with race is at play in the new division arising among South Africa's youth: apartheid's children *versus* democracy's children. Many young black people … use a racially dichotomous language in which those who are not seen as "truly" black are referred to as "coconuts" – black youth, most likely from Model C schools, who are seen to speak, dress and act like white people; while those seen to inhabit a "backward blackness" – rural ways of being and/or black youth who seem to be stuck in "old struggle politics" – are called "dusty-crusties"'. Zimitri Erasmus, 'Race and Identity in the Nation', in *State of the Nation: South Africa 2004–2005*, ed. John Daniel et al. (Cape Town: HSRC Press, 2005), 27.
45 Steyn and van Zyl, '"Like that Statue at Jammie Stairs"', executive summary, n.p.
46 See, notably, Pierre Bourdieu and Jean-Claude Passeron, *Reproduction in Education, Society and Culture*, trans. R. Nice (Oxford: Blackwell, 1990).
47 Bourdieu *In Other Words*, 11.
48 For a useful survey of staff attitudes towards race at historically white universities – but one whose argument perhaps also calls for the deployment of a concept of cultural capital to strengthen its analytic reach and explanatory power – see Nomthandazo S. Gwele, 'Racial relations in selected faculties in English-language historically white universities in South Africa', *Society in Transition* 33, no. 1 (2002): 134–51. The survey raises the question – without addressing it directly – of whether differences of *habitus* can be used as evidence for active racism. For a useful explication of the concept of *habitus*, see Bourdieu, *The Logic of Practice*, 52–79.
49 For a useful discussion of the complications of class versus racial analysis in South African historiography, see Neville Alexander's essay, 'Race and Class in South African Historiography' in Neville Alexander, *An Ordinary Country* (Scottsville: University of Natal Press, 2002). In a frustrated moment, Alexander concludes that 'in the final analysis, it is empirical research that is required to give an approximation of the relationship between race (or gender, or ethnic group, etc.) and class, rather than any reductionist forumula

derived from abstract models of society' (25). Erasmus's key phrase – 'racialized inequality' – may offer the most useful distinction (Erasmus, *State of the Nation*).

50 Meanwhile, left-liberal multiculturalism 'emphasizes cultural differences and suggests that the stress on the quality of races smothers those important cultural differences between races that are responsible for different behaviours, values, attitudes, cognitive styles, and social practices' (McLaren, 'White Terror and Oppositional Agency', 51). For McLaren, it tends to 'exoticize "otherness" in a nativist retreat that locates difference in a primeval past of cultural authenticity', a retreat that at the same time authorises a 'populist elitism' in which 'one's own location as an oppressed person is supposed to offer a special authority from which to speak'. While not arguing against 'the importance of experience in the formation of political identity', McLaren is wary of the ways in which an appeal to experience 'has become the new imprimatur for legitimating the political currency and incontestable validity of one's arguments'. 'This', he concludes, 'has often resulted in a reverse form of academic elitism' (52).

51 Recent research suggests that the limits of this are becoming ever-more apparent. See, for instance, Catherine Bargh, Peter Scott and David Smith, *Governing Universities: Changing the Culture?* (Buckingham: Open University Press, 1996): 'the government has encouraged the belief that the corporate sector provides the most appropriate model of governance for higher education in the age of massification and marketization' (167). 'The discussion of recent developments in corporate governance suggests that this second assertion should be treated with considerable caution … there is little evidence to suggest that the corporate sector has useful models of governance to offer higher education' (167), and again, the '(perhaps obsessive) focus has been on more effective management, which has been interpreted as an elevation of the managerial interest at the expense of professional perspectives' (168).

52 Readings, *The University in Ruins*, 3, and see especially 21–43.

53 'Programme for Higher Education Transformation', Education Draft White Paper 3 (Pretoria: Department of Education, 1997), 1.

54 Immanuel Kant, 'An Answer to the Question: "What is Enlightenment?"', in Immanuel Kant, *Political Writings*, ed. H. Reiss, trans. H.B. Nisbet (Cambridge: Cambridge University Press, 1991). For a useful discussion of Kant's contribution to the formation of the very idea of public opinion, see especially Jurgen Habermas, *The Structural Transformation of the Public Sphere*, trans. Thomas Burger with the assistance of Frederick Lawrence (Oxford: Polity Press, 1992), 102–117; see also Derrida's informative and provocative discussion, 'Mochlos ou le conflit des Facultés' in Jacques Derrida, *Du Droit à la Philosophie* (Paris: Galilée, 1990). For an interesting recent highlighting of the complexities and antinomies within Kant's position, see Stathis Kouvelakis, *Philosophy and Revolution: From Kant to Marx* (London and New York: Verso, 2003), especially 12–23.

55 'Programme for Higher Education Transformation', 1.

56 Edgar H. Schein, *Organizational Culture and Leadership: A Dynamic View* (San Francisco: Jossey-Bass, [1975] 1985), 2.

57 Trish Gibbon and Jane Kabaki, 'Staff' in Cloete *et al.* (eds), *Transformation in Higher Education*, 217.

58 Gibbon and Kabaki, 'Staff', 217.

59 Gibbon and Kabaki, 'Staff', 218.

60 Gibbon and Kabaki, 'Staff', 216.

61 Olajide Oloyede, 'Disciplinary Cultures and Academic Leadership', *Society in Transition* 33, no. X (2002), 116–33. For a useful comparative argument, also locating the new managerialism firmly in the imperatives of the post-Reagan neo-liberalism, see C.F.S. Chachage, 'Higher Education Transformation and Academic Exterminism', CODESRIA

Bulletin nos 1–2 (2001): 6. Summing up the changes introduced by the new managerialism, Chachage charges that they amounted to 'a call for the "market" to dictate biases in universities. Thus, there would be a bias for professional as opposed to liberal faculties and within faculties a bias for the imparting of "technical" skills rather than critical analytical ones' (4).

62 Oloyede, 'Disciplinary Cultures and Academic Leadership', 118.
63 Oloyede, 'Disciplinary Cultures and Academic Leadership', 117.
64 For a fuller discussion, see Higgins, 'Institutional Culture as Keyword'.
65 See Ensor, 'Curriculum', in *Transformation in Higher Education*. Ensor's conclusion regarding the success of programmes illustrates the difficult dynamics of institutional culture from any instrumentalist perspective. The National Council on Higher Education had sought to impose from above academic programmes that sought to promote the managerial virtues of 'interdisciplinarity, portability, coherence and responsiveness'. To the question 'has this been achieved?', Ensor's answer is 'unequivocally "no" in respect of portability, but with respect to the others, contingent upon how one defines an academic programme and the descriptors involved' (287–88). Despite this sugaring of the pill ('contingent upon how one defines an academic programme'), Ensor's article makes clear that the response to the perceived imposition of programmes revealed levels of an academic culture still strong enough to resist change when regarded as pedagogically inappropriate. Indeed, as Ensor ultimately concedes, 'the central organizing principle of university undergraduate curricula remains the disciplines. In this sense, contemporary curricula in sciences and humanities look little different from the way they did before academic programme implementation began' (289).
66 Henry Louis Gates, 'Good-Bye, Columbus? Notes on the Culture of Criticism', in Goldberg (ed.), *Multiculturalism: A Critical Reader*, 206.
67 Erasmus, 'Race and Identity in the Nation', 20.
68 Erasmus, 'Race and Identity in the Nation', 27.
69 Erasmus, 'Race and Identity in the Nation', 30. More broadly, Mahmood Mamdani has recently noted, 'Africa's real political challenge is to reform and thus sublate the form of the state that has continued to reproduce race and ethnicity as political identities'; it is 'to create a single political community and citizenship from diverse cultural historical groups and identities'. Mahmood Mamdani, 'Race and Identity as Political Identities in the African Context' in *Keywords: Identity*, ed. N. Tazi. (Cape Town: Double Storey, 2004), 22. In similar mode, Neville Alexander warns against all forms of 'ethnic mobilisation', and suggests that the 'real challenge' for South Africa 'lies in moving away from the notion (and the reality) of separate racial, and to some extent also ethnic, groups towards a situation where the multiculturalism of the society can find its expression in the fact of multiple identities of the individual held together by an overarching national identity' (Alexander, *An Ordinary Country*, 98).
70 For a useful discussion of such displacement, see Bourdieu et al., *The Weight of the World*, 620–21.
71 Williams, *Keywords*, 91.

Reviews

Hywel Dix, *After Raymond Williams: Cultural Materialism and the Breakup of Britain*. University of Wales Press, 2008. xvi + 192 pp. £18.99 pb. ISBN 978-0-7083-2153-9

The British election of 2010 was notable for many things: the eventual election of a Coalition government; the choice of an Old Etonian as Prime Minister for the first time since the 1960s; Conservative dominance in England against a relative absence in Wales and especially in Scotland; the failure of the Scottish National Party to prosper despite its minority control of the Scottish Assembly. Residual and emerging political and social forces clearly were in play. How well the Coalition holds together is something for future historians, but the potential for acrimonious division remains high. What seems unlikely in the short term, though, is a political breakup of Britain in any cataclysmic sense. That being so, the subtitle of Hywel Dix's *After Raymond Williams: Cultural Materialism and the Breakup of Britain* might appear challenged by events on the ground. But the book, published in 2008, argues for an historical tendency towards breakup rather than any imminent division of Britain. The title of Williams's own *The Long Revolution* cautions against the hope or fear that substantial and lasting change happens cataclysmically, and Dix resists overcooking his case, especially as his primary interest lies not in political structures and affiliations but in the ways that writing, film and culture contribute to and critically analyse established notions of national identity and unity. His study comes 'after' Williams both in the sense of summarising and scrutinising Williams's voluminous writing and in considering the evolving (or, better, devolving) state of Britain in the decades since Williams's death in 1988. That year neatly falls between Wales's rejection of self-rule in 1979 and its embracing of devolution in 1997, Dix arguing that this difference marks that nation's increased cultural confidence, something that Williams had done much to foster. As part of the 'Writing Wales in English' series published by the University of Wales Press, *After Raymond Williams* reflects and plays its own small part in sustaining and developing that self-confidence. More generally, Dix argues, changes in Wales's sense of its own identity represent a broader challenge to what he, following Williams, sees as a now-obsolete unitary British state.

    This ambitious account draws from the vast corpus of work by Williams to focus on a particular, substantial and consistent element: 'the relationship between writing and the breakup of Britain'. Dix convincingly shows the importance of this relationship to Williams's theoretical and creative writing over the whole of his career, examining the development of key concepts and approaches in such diverse areas as the Welsh industrial novel, the function of universities and certain films starring Hugh Grant. Clearly Williams himself wrote provocatively on the first two subjects but was not alive to experience the rise of Grant's particularly successful portrayal of what Dix classifies as the 'English buffoon', but the inclusion of figures such as Grant demonstrates how Dix attempts to apply Williams's ideas to more recent cultural phenomena. Two clear points of reference from within Williams's lifetime are Tom Nairn's *The Breakup of Britain* and Benedict Anderson's *Imagined Communities*, which offer suggestive, historically embedded, critiques of notions of nationhood. Dix usefully works through points of overlap and difference, allying Williams more with Anderson's concentration on the imaginative construction of nationhood than Nairn's position that Scotland's status as a nation pre-dating the Act of Union undermines England's hegemony. For Anderson, as for Williams, nations and the relationships between them are works in progress, especially in the case of Britain where imbalances of political, financial and cultural power have had such a defining role. What Williams strove to uncover and analyse was how cultural production was vital to the ongoing and contested narration of nations, something that not only encompassed the past but also constructed imaginative accounts of other possibilities, of alternative futures.

Dix also works to place Williams's ideas in a larger arena of cultural debate populated by such diverse thinkers as Sigmund Freud, T.S. Eliot, Homi Bhabha, Julia Kristeva and Laura Mulvey. In part this effort reflects positively on the sweep and significance of Williams's large (though admittedly sometimes uneven) body of work, and Dix gives a convincing explanation of the ways in which Williams continued to refine his thinking, partly in response to other critics, across a diverse array of topics. It remains sometimes unclear, though, whether the links Dix establishes between Williams and other figures are instances of actual intellectual engagement by Williams with those thinkers or merely interesting and illuminating points of comparison. Yet the book's central focus on the makeup and breakup of Britain counteracts any tendency to give equal weight to the whole corpus. This sensible and necessary concentration still allows for a fair degree of scope, for instance allowing Dix to discuss Williams's interest in the role of traditional universities as purveyors of traditional conceptions of knowledge and national identity. Dix contrasts prescriptive 'hard' universities that transmit limited and limiting 'truths' with 'soft' universities that encourage inquisitive scepticism; this acts as a means of categorising Williams's own open-ended approach to intellectual inquiry and to political engagement. He also explores Williams's work on imperialism from *The Country and the City* onwards, relating it to more recent postcolonial discussion. The thoughtful treatment of this wealth of material does not mean that the book fashions an uncritical assessment: Dix recognises Williams's relative blind spot to radical feminism, and the question mark in the title of the concluding chapter, 'Postmodern Williams?' seems well-advised.

While covering a substantial amount of Williams's theoretical and critical work, the study also deals with his novels, presenting sustained interpretations of works such as *Border Country*, *The Fight for Manod* and *The Volunteers* within chapters dealing with the Welsh industrial novel, the campus novel, and postcolonialism. Again, the intersection of these creative texts and broader social contexts and issues points to Williams's efforts to see fiction as contributing materially to the making and critical consideration of society. Dix connects the established and elitist campus novel and other works by 'Movement' writers with a political conservatism underpinning an already outdated belief in the unitary nation state, something that Williams's own novels called into question. He sees in more recent Scottish and Welsh fiction the continuation of that questioning of national identity within and between Britain's constituent nations, listing a powerful assortment of contemporary Scottish and Welsh writers such as Niall Griffiths, Janice Galloway, Irvine Welsh and Trezza Azzopardi whom he believes to be engaged in fashioning these new representations. Although Dix explains that 'full analysis is not possible here' of those recent writers the lack of follow-through is frustrating. The same is true for the chapter on film. Dix notes Williams's early interest in the medium, looking at the development of the concept of 'flow'. But the importance of Williams's contribution to film theory and film criticism remains far less significant than his undoubted influence on literary studies and on other literary critics. Dix makes interesting assessments of some of Hugh Grant's films in terms of English middle-class identity, but again the range of recent films that he rightly argues 'carry out a renegotiation of British identity' are more listed than analysed. These quibbles do not invalidate the arguments Dix makes, but rather point to the difficulties of accounting comprehensively for Williams's richness and diversity. Dix makes a strong case for the important interaction of writing and national identity generally in that work, and for the role writing and (to a lesser extent) film continue to play in the ongoing negotiation of that identity. And he successfully shows how Williams's general approach incorporates a sceptical open-endedness that constantly raises necessary questions, whether on the history, current state and future of writing or of national unity. Ultimately, Dix opens up the question of the place Williams's ideas will or might have in the 21st century. Through brief, suggestive sketches of recent writing and film he makes a tantalising start to work that he seems eminently qualified to pursue. We can only look forward to finding out what Dix himself produces after *After Raymond Williams*.

Peter Marks
University of Sydney

Stefania Michelucci, *The Poetry of Thom Gunn: A Critical Study*. Jefferson, NC & London: McFarland & Company, 2009. 222pp. n.p. pb. ISBN 978-0-7864-3687-3

Like any book-length study of our major poets, Stefania Michelucci's overview of Thom Gunn is a welcome violation of the usual silence. Translated from the Italian, her book is scrupulously researched, and Gunn's volumes are systematically presented in it. There is an interesting diversion on Gunn and Caravaggio; and she pays a lot of attention to the 1966 collection *Positives* – in which Gunn's short poems accompanied photographs by his brother – even if she has to acknowledge its palpable weaknesses. However, despite being an obvious enthusiast for his work, she often seems to miss the point.

In her approach to the early poems about masculinity Michelucci is barely more comfortable with Gunn's choices of topic than his original reviewers were, back in the 1960s. It is an overstatement to claim that *The Sense of Movement* 'pulsates with violent heroes'. But you can understand how she reaches this conclusion when you see what she considers violent. The mere riding of motorbikes, in 'On the Move', and the incidental scaring of some birds, is described as 'a violent action'.

Gunn was a man with a serious sense of humour, but Michelucci often does not get it. When reading those early poems she sees the will but not the wit. She claims that 'Even in bed I pose', the famous opening line of 'Carnal Knowledge', is an 'icy line', without conveying any sense of the joy that suffuses a beautifully playful poem. Similarly, she speaks of the 'chilling lines' of 'Lines for my 55th Birthday' without noticing that the poem is, or contains, a joke. Occasionally, language is the problem. When commenting on 'Lofty in the Palais de Danse' Michelucci appreciates the denotations of the nickname (dignified, proud) but overlooks its ironic reference to height: Lofty is either very tall or, more probably, rather short. The translator from the Italian, apparently unaware that Balzac was French, leaves in a reference to his novel *Papà Goriot*. A slip-up in the translation suggests that Gunn's last volume was 'dedicated to' the serial killer Jeffrey Dahmer, which is not the case. But these are routine problems of cultural distance and not many of them crop up.

Although she tries to face up to it, Michelucci seems uncomfortable with Gunn's sexuality. A four-page section called 'Gay Pride' gives up on gayness after two pages. Her sense of whether Gunn was a 'gay poet' is expressed in the crudest of terms: 'The choice of a heterosexual couple' as a topic for 'The Discovery of the Pacific' in *Moly* 'confirms the poet's refusal to be identified solely as a gay poet who writes for a specific, exclusive audience'. I can't think of any gay poet who does do that; and I can't imagine a world in which gay writers, like gay people in general, would have nothing to say about heterosexuals. And yet, when she writes about the gender-unspecified poem 'The Hug', she treats it solely as a poem about 'homosexuality'. Her remarks about AIDS in the appended interview with Gunn, conducted in 1990, actually made me gasp in embarrassment. Gunn responded, though, with his usual equanimity.

Nowhere is there any sign that the costumes, poses and paraphernalia of sadomasochistic play might represent not violence, but the performance of violence; not pathology, but a posture. If we follow the common line, that 'in the early collections, subconscious repression of his homosexuality caused sadomasochistic attitudes and poses' that then gave way to greater tenderness (as Michelucci does), we shall overlook the fact that Gunn was a cheerful – and tender – participant in the leather/SM subculture of his adopted city. Michelucci complains that in his last volume, *Boss Cupid*, Gunn 'changes Cupid … into a tyrant'. But since when was the little blighter anything else? Is there any significant literature about love that has portrayed him otherwise? Gunn's Cupid, like all his paradoxical versions of love, springs from a long tradition. At some point, Michelucci has lost track of the fact that, for all that he was gay and became an American, Gunn wrote at the centre of the English mainstream, as a traditionalist social radical.

Michelucci's is a conventional approach, doggedly following the critical reception, and seemingly unwilling to depart from it. She often reads the poems as if she were just encountering them for the first time. Of course, this might, at times, result in an engaging spontaneity of response. But the actual consequence is that the whole book reads like an introductory primer, its attention to individual poems as often dutiful as engaged. That said, an introductory primer to a major poet is not unwelcome: all school and university libraries should order it.

Gregory Woods
Nottingham Trent University

Jack Jones, *Black Parade*. Cardigan: Parthian Books, 2009. xiv + 414 pp. £8.99 pb. ISBN 978-1-906998-14-1

The writing career of Jack Jones (1884–1970) strikingly combined breadth across genres and media with a firm rootedness in Welsh industrial experience. In total he produced eleven novels, a trilogy of autobiographical volumes, and numerous plays for stage, radio and screen. Despite the critical and commercial success he once enjoyed, of late Jones's work has slipped from view. Until recently, all of his novels were out of print; in the period since Raymond Williams's engagement with Jones's fiction in the essay 'The Welsh Industrial

Novel' (1979), Jones has been largely overlooked by criticism committed to recovering and analysing formations of working-class writing.

The re-issue of Jones's second novel, *Black Parade* (1935), in the Library of Wales series, is therefore especially welcome. Committed to recovering 'unjustly neglected' Welsh writing in English, the series has so far re-published significant working-class novels including *Cwmardy* (1937) and *We Live* (1939) by Jack Jones's contemporary and namesake, the Rhondda Communist Party activist Lewis Jones (1897–1939). For Raymond Williams, whose own debut novel *Border Country* (1960) also appears in the series, both Joneses were engaged in a creative struggle to find fictional forms appropriate for working-class experience. Working-class structures of feeling and ways of seeing, Williams notes in 'The Welsh Industrial Novel', historically found little of use in the plot devices of conventional fiction – 'the propertied marriage and settlement; the intricacies of inheritance; the exotic adventure; the abstracted romance'.[1] For working-class writers, narrating the story of a 'typical' *family* provided one answer to these 'acute compositional difficulties', offering a route into 'central common experiences'. '[W]hat is really being written', Williams continues, 'is the story of a class; indeed effectively, given the local historical circumstances, of a people' (223). In one variant of this pattern, he observes, the dispersal of the family – as members emigrate under the pressures of economic hardship – creates elegiac resonances. In others, as in Lewis Jones's ideologically driven novels, the family breakup is narrated more positively: family ties are willingly subordinated and loyalties transferred to the larger collective of a political cause.

Black Parade takes a different line on the family novel, overcoming what Williams calls the 'black despair of locality' (226) potentially encircling a family narrative by extending the frame historically, plotting the family's endurance through several generations. Set in Jones's hometown of Merthyr Tydfil, the novel tracks four generations of the Morgan family between the late 1880s and early 1930s. The central characters are Saran, who works in the brickyards prior to marrying the heavy-drinking collier Glyn Morgan, and her wayward brother Harry, whose days of loose-living and bare-knuckle street-fighting are stopped in their tracks after religious conversion. Jones's novel presents a powerful and engrossing panorama of industrial working-class community through decades of profound economic, political, social and cultural change. *Black Parade* records the restructuring of capital and labour through the period, as individual pit owners combine into larger companies and the miners

Note

1   Raymond Williams, 'The Welsh Industrial Novel' (1979), reprinted in *Problems in Materialism and Culture* (London and New York: Verso, 1980), 219. Page references are hereafter given in parenthesis in the text.

develop their Federation. It charts political shifts as the younger generation turn from Lloyd George and the Liberals to the parties of organised labour (the Independent Labour Party, the Labour Party and the Communist Party). The novel is equally attuned to the transformation of working-class cultural habits, notably the decline of popular theatre as the cinema takes hold.

In the novel's strongest sections, such changes are not an unpicturesque backdrop but a shaping force lived to the very fibres of the community's being. As Williams notes, this quality distinguishes Jones's novel from the reductive 'sentimental figuration' of the same historical period in Richard Llewellyn's *How Green Was My Valley* (1939), the 'export version of the Welsh industrial experience' (227). But while, as Williams points out, the strength of *Black Parade* lies precisely in 'the many-sided turbulence, the incoherence and contradictions, which the more available stereotypes of the history exclude' (226), this stimulating polyphony of views and voices is more apparent in the novel's earlier sections, which deal with the pre-First World War period, than with the later, in which the novel rushes the story up to Jones's present. In the thinning of these final sections it is possible to detect a tension between the novel's intuitive materialism, which registers the constitutive force of 'context' and implies the need for structural change, and Jones's own political trajectory, which in the 1920s and early 1930s moved restlessly rightwards through the Communist Party, the Labour Party, and the Liberal Party before culminating in a short-lived sympathy for Oswald Mosley's New Party. Saran's perspective – that of a hard-bitten survivor who has seen interchangeable politicians come and go – increasingly dominates the narrative. In the section dealing with the General Strike, for instance, the narrative is filtered through her perspective; one scene samples but abruptly cuts short the radical critique and call for solidarity articulated by miners' leader A.J. Cook. ('I've heard all I want to hear', Saran comments, before leaving the mass meeting where Cook is speaking.) Mirroring the overarching narrative, the emphasis here turns away from collective solutions towards individual responsibility – looking after self and family – the 'common sense' popular ideology which Saran increasingly embodies. But if such moments conflict with the logic of the preceding narrative, imposing closure and conclusions rather than drawing them out, they are also a reminder that *Black Parade*, like many working-class novels, is less a coherent text than the location of a process, a search for meaning and narrative form. The Library of Wales is to be congratulated for restoring to view the contradictory richness of Jones's novel in this scholarly, handsomely presented and affordable edition.

Ben Harker
University of Salford

Peter Brooker and Andrew Thacker (eds), *The Oxford Critical and Cultural History of Modernist Magazines. Volume 1. Britain and Ireland: 1880–1955.* Oxford: Oxford University Press, 2009, xvii + 955pp. £80 hb. ISBN 978-0-19-921115-9

Hundreds of 'little magazines' committed to new and experimental writing sprang up in the early decades of the twentieth century. The adjective 'little' applied neither to their physical size, nor the scale of their artistic ambitions, but to the material conditions of publication. Indifferent to, or even contemptuous of, commercial considerations, the editors of little magazines typically set out their stalls at the margins of literary culture, promoting the activities of artistic communities dedicated to literary and artistic reform, and seeking out small elite readerships. Financially unviable, they seldom lasted long. As Malcolm Cowley has quipped, 'the history of a little magazine is summarized in its format. The first issue consists, let us say, of sixty-four pages, with half tone illustrations, printed on coated paper. The second has sixty-four pages, illustrated with line cuts. The third has only forty-eight pages; the fourth has thirty-two, without illustrations; the fifth never appears.'

However, so-called 'little magazines' assumed cultural importance disproportionate to their name. In a great age of manifestos, short-lived publications catered to shifting aesthetic allegiances and provided a lively forum for new talent, publishing now celebrated writers such as Ezra Pound, T.S. Eliot, James Joyce, D.H. Lawrence and Wyndham Lewis before their work became acceptable to the mainstream. As Pound stated, 'as he looked back on high modernism from the vantage point of the 1930s, 'The history of contemporary letters has, to a very manifest extent, been written in such magazines'. Yet the formative role of magazines in early twentieth-century literature and art has scarcely received the critical attention it deserves. Scholarship has tended to be confined to a limited range of Anglophone little magazines, and our understanding of modernism has been impoverished for it, until now.

The Oxford Critical and Cultural History of Modernist Magazines: Britain and Ireland: 1880–1955, the first instalment in a three-volume series, edited by Peter Brooker and Andrew Thacker, offers by far the fullest account of modernist magazines to date, expanding beyond little reviews to 'the far more diverse spectrum of periodicals in which modernist work first appeared'. Providing fresh perspectives on over 80 periodicals, including time-honoured publications such as *The New Age*, *The English Review*, *The Egoist*, *The Criterion*, *New Verse* and *Horizon*, as well as accounts of relatively neglected ventures such as *Voices*, *Form*, *The Acorn*, *Coterie* and *The Apple*, and curios that folded after one issue, such as *Arson*, *Klaxon* and *Daylight*, this groundbreaking volume firmly establishes the foundational role that periodicals played in the rise of literary and artistic modernism. It contains 37 chapters by some of the most important and original interpreters of modernist culture working today, and is arranged into ten historically themed sections, accompanied by incisive and wide-ranging introductions by Brooker and Thacker.

Raymond Williams's discussions of hegemony and foundations provide the conceptual framework and 'cultural vocabulary' for this enterprise. As Brooker and Thacker observe, Williams's 'distinction between "dominant", "residual" and "emergent" cultural tendencies or practices has at the outset a flexibility that other more static identifications of the unitary character of cultural epochs […] do not have'. Williams's method and vocabulary thus provide the contributors with 'a way of describing the relations of magazines to a hegemonic mainstream as an active and changing set of relationships' that helps to 'identify "residual" and "emergent" emphases *within* single magazines or across the career of a changing title, group, or generation'. Reaching back as far as the Pre-Raphaelite Brotherhood organ *The Germ*, and as far forward as Cyril Connolly's *Horizon*, *The Oxford Critical and Cultural History* succeeds admirably in delineating the rise of modernist culture in its multiple forms from many of its scattered points of origin to the later critical formation of an institutionalised version of modernism in reviews such as *Scrutiny*.

True to the conception of a critical and cultural history, the essays are comparative in spirit, recovering the debates and dialogues sustained across rival magazines or exploring phases in social, political and aesthetic orientation of single reviews. Close attention of this kind proves revisionary, as demonstrated by the three chapters that compose Part IV, entitled 'Transitions'. In a fine essay that steers between two opposing views of the modernity and importance of *The New Age*, a broadly socialist review of politics and arts, Ann Ardis exposes 'the machinery of selective tradition' that powers arguments about magazines' places in literary and cultural history. She shows how *The New Age* under A.R. Orage formed 'an important venue for avant-garde publication in London during the pre-war period', but also subjected experimental literature and art to intense criticism in its extended commentaries on other magazines. Critical of the 'economies of connoisseurship and patronage' that supported the modernist avant-garde, Ardis argues, *The New Age* refused to identify exclusively with any 'periodical community', marketed itself to 'a rising middle-class readership' and strove to sustain 'unbounded and open-ended' debate. Ardis's essay is followed by Cliff Wulfmann's illuminating history of *The English Review*, as 'a fountainhead of modernism' in the fifteen months it was edited by Ford Madox Ford, revealing its origins in the Edwardian period and charting its decline in the post-Ford years, when 'the focus shifted from *belles-lettres* to politics' and 'adult' material, and then again in 1923 when it was taken over by a series of increasingly conservative editors, becoming an organ of the extreme right-wing in 1936, before failing in 1937. The section closes with a provocative, but persuasive, reassessment of *The London Mercury*, a hugely popular neo-Georgian weekly edited by J.C. Squire, that is traditionally understood as a stoutly conservative, market-driven, middlebrow publication that sought 'to squelch the modernist movement'. While Squire was certainly not above claiming that Wyndham Lewis's short-lived Vorticist review *Blast* folded 'shortly after a hostile critic, consulting his Webster, had discovered the definition: "Blast: – a flatulent disease of sheep"' or musing that the Dadaist magazine *391* costs 'two francs, but this figure may be possibly one of the poems', J. Matthew Huculak reminds us that *The London Mercury* published 'the poetry and prose of W.B. Yeats, Robert Graves, Virginia Woolf, Katherine Mansfield, a young Dorothy Sayers', and American authors such as Willa Cather, Edith Wharton and Sherwood Anderson.

Essays of this quality, unseating tired but commonly held views of modernist literature and culture (such as the much cited distinction between Georgians and Edwardians so vividly sketched in 'Mr. Bennett and Mrs. Brown'), populate *The Oxford Critical and Cultural History*. Whereas early studies of modernist magazines focused on the forum they provided for canonical male authors, many of this volume's contributors quietly assert the active, and in many cases leading, roles female writers, intellectuals and editors played in modernist periodical culture. Jane Dowson's thoughtful and meticulously researched discussion of the ways in which *Time and Tide* and *The Bermondsey Book* 'promoted the social equality of women and the working class' is exemplary in this respect. Far from setting up 'alternative subcultures of minority groups', Dowson shows the contribution these two publications made to what Habermas terms the public 'exchange of ideas'. Other highlights of the volume include, but are by no means limited to: Peter Brooker's essay on John Middleton Murry's early reviews, *Rhythm*, *The Blue Review* and *The Signature*; Jason Harding and Michael Whitworth's affirmations of the vision and reach of Eliot and Middleton Murry in their role as editors; the set of essays on the wide-ranging concerns of 1920s periodicals (including a fascinating essay by Thacker on the clusters of writers involved in *Coterie*, *New Coterie* and *The Owl*); Stan Smith's discussion of *New Verse*; and Sean Matthews' essay on *Scrutiny* (which, in keeping with the Cambridge interest in aesthetic form, playfully references all twenty volumes).

Additionally, over 100 images – including many striking covers – sharply map aesthetic transitions in the period from the floridities of *fin-de-siècle* quarterlies to the stylised nudes by John Duncan Ferguson and Anne Estelle Rice that dressed the pages of *Rhythm* or the dignified sobriety of Eliot's review *The Criterion*. Responding to the 'materialist turn' in modernist studies, *The*

Reviews

Oxford Critical and Cultural History is packed with information about how periodicals addressed themselves to their markets, from their page layout, typefaces, paper quality, binding, and price, to their use and placement of advertisements, and their networks of distribution and sales, and while this information is telling in and of itself, a few of the weaker contributions fail to show what such a knowledge adds to our understanding of the political, literary and aesthetic discourses that mark contributions to modernist magazines.

The penultimate section, 'Beyond the Metropolis', contains illuminating essays by Chris Hopkins, Frank Shovlin, Cairns Craig, Olga Taxidou and Mark Jacobs which call attention to regional publications such as *The Welsh Review* or *The Voice of Scotland* and their distinctive, but marginalised, contributions to the literary culture of the time. Having considered magazines of the Celtic Revival such as *Beltaine* and *Dana*, and the activities of members of the Leeds Art Club in earlier essays, the decision that the section on Welsh and Scottish magazines should stand outside the chronological design of the book confirms that regional modernisms remain peripheral to critical evaluations of the period. The geographical reach of *The Oxford Critical and Cultural History* is extended further still in very last essay of the collection to include James Keery's interesting and valuable coda on *Indian Writing*, a magazine 'deeply involved in the complex developments between the birth of Indian modernism and the aftermath of independence'. Keery concludes with a rumination on the destiny of India, which is right in the context of the essay, but an odd note to end the whole volume, and a further editorial statement summarising the force of the volume's contribution to modernist scholarship would have been welcome. Such a statement may come in the second and third volumes, on America and Europe, which will be eagerly awaited by readers interested in modernism and/or periodical culture.

Sarah Davison
University of Nottingham

Raymond Williams Foundation (RWF)

Formerly the Raymond Williams Memorial Fund, the RWF has among its aims 'to commemorate the works of Raymond Williams, in particular in the sphere of adult education for the benefit of the public'. The RWF had a good year in 2009–2010 with successful activities across several spheres.

The 22nd annual Raymond Williams weekend took place in May 2010. The theme was *Towards 2020* (loosely based on Williams's book *Towards 2000*). The keynote lecture by Michael Rustin on the Friday evening, 7th May (the day after the General Election) was an analysis of the current economic and political developments. It is now available on the RWF website along with contributions to the weekend by Granville Williams on T*he Manufacture of Consent* and Malcolm Pittock on *The Long Revolution*. The 23rd weekend will be held at the Wedgwood Memorial College (WMC) on 6th–8th May 2011. The theme will be *The Spirit Level*, based on the recent book by Frank Wilkinson and Kate Pickett.[1]

RWF helped fund fifteen projects over the year including a Cuba Day; a Workers Educational Association (WEA) weekly *Issues in Politics* course; the Cambridge Women's Resource Centre; and Oldham Unity's education work with refugees and asylum seekers.

These are obviously exceptionally difficult times for adult education but RWF's projects offer practical, cost-effective ways forward. We are now involved in the new Co-operative Movement /WEA partnership which builds upon 'Co-op and WEA shared values of active citizenship, democracy and equality'.

Derek Tatton
RWF Administrator and RWS Executive Committee Member.
www.raymondwilliamsfoundation.org.uk

Note
1 Richard Wilkinson and Kate Pickett, *The Spirit Level: Why More Equal Societies Almost Always Do Better* (London: Allen Lane, 2009).

Style Notes for Contributors

Presentation of Copy
Key Words is an internationally refereed academic journal. In the first instance typescripts for prospective publication should be submitted to the Contributions Editor (details may be found on the inside back cover). Articles should normally be no longer than 6,000 words; reviews should typically be between 1,500 and 2,000 words. Articles should be double spaced, with generous margins, and pages should be numbered consecutively. For matters of style not addressed below, please refer to *The Chicago Manual of Style*, 15th edn or http://www.chicagomanualofstyle.org/contents.html. Contributors who fail to observe these notes may be asked to revise their submission in accordance with them.

Provision of Text in Electronic Format
Key Words is prepared electronically. Consequently, contributors whose work is accepted for publication will be asked to supply a file copy of their work (either on disc, CD-ROM or by electronic mail) to the Contributions Editor. The preferred word processing format is Microsoft Word (any version).

References and Bibliographic Conventions
Citations in *Key Words* appear as endnotes at the conclusion of each contribution. Essays presented for prospective publication should adopt this style. Endnote markers should be given in arabic numerals and positioned after, not before, punctuation marks, e.g. '.1' rather than '1.'. With no bibliography, full details must be given in a note at the first mention of any work cited. Subsequent citations can then use the short form or a cross-reference. Headline-style capitalisation is used. In headline style, the first and last words of title and subtitle and all other major words are capitalised. Titles of books and journals should be formatted in italics (not underlined).

Please cite books in the following manner:

On first citation: Raymond Williams and Michael Orrom, *Preface to Film* (London: Film Drama, 1954).

On subsequent citations: Williams and Orrom, *Preface to Film*, 12.

Please cite journal articles in the following manner:

Patrick Parrinder, 'Politics, Letters and the National Curriculum', *Changing English* 2, no. 1 (1994): 29.

Chapters in books should be referenced in the following way:

Andrew McRae, 'The Peripatetic Muse: Internal Travel and the Cultural Production of Space in Pre-Revolutionary England', in *The Country and the City Revisited: England and the Politics of Culture, 1550–1850*, ed. Gerald MacLean, Donna Landry, and Joseph P. Ward (Cambridge: Cambridge University Press, 1999), 41–57.

For internet articles:

Raymond Williams Society Executive, 'About the Raymond Williams Society', Raymond Williams Society, http://www.raymondwilliams.co.uk/ (accessed 26 March 2009).

Please refer to newspaper articles in the following way:

John Mullan, 'Rebel in a Tweed Suit', *The Observer*, 28 May 2005, Features and Reviews section, 37.

A thesis should be referenced in the following manner:

E. Allen, 'The Dislocated Mind: The Fictions of Raymond Williams' (PhD diss., Liverpool John Moores University, 2007), 22–9.

Conference papers should be cited in the following style:

Dai Smith, 'Translating Raymond Williams' (paper presented at the Raymond Williams's Culture and Society@50 conference, Canolfan Dylan Thomas Centre, Swansea, 7 November 2008).

Quotations

For quotations use single quotation marks, and double quotation marks for quotations within quotations. Punctuation is used outside quotations.. Ensure that all spellings, punctuation, abbreviations etc. within a quotation are rendered exactly as in the original, including errors, which should be signalled by the authorial interpolation '(*sic*)'.

Style Notes for Contributors

Books Received

Book reviews should open with full bibliographic details of the text under review. These details should include (in the following order): in bold type, first name(s) and surname(s) of author(s), or first name(s) and surname(s) of editor(s) followed by a parenthetic '(ed.)' or '(eds); in italics, the full title of the volume followed by a period and a hard return; then, in regular type, the place of publication, publisher and date of publication; the page extent of the volume, including front papers numbered in Roman numerals; the price (where available) of the supplied copy and an indication of 'pb.' or 'hb.'; and the ISBN of the supplied copy. For example:

Dai Smith, *Raymond Williams: A Warriors Tale.*
Parthian Books, 2008. xviii + 514 pp. £24.99 hb. ISBN 978 1 905762 56 9.